Dead Ahead

The Web Dilemma
and the New Rules of Business

Dead Ahead

The Web Dilemma
and the New Rules of Business

by

Laurie Windham

with Jon Samsel

ALLWORTH PRESS
NEW YORK

04 03 02 01 00 99   5 4 3 2 1

Published by Allworth Press
An imprint of Allworth Communications
10 East 23rd Street, New York, NY 10010

Cover design by Douglas Design Associates, New York, NY

Page composition/typography by SR Desktop Services, Ridge, NY

Library of Congress Cataloging-in-Publication Data
Windham, Laurie.
    Dead ahead: the Web dilemma and the new rules of business /
Laurie Windham with Jon Samsel.
        p.   cm.
    Includes index.
    ISBN: 1-58115-033-4 (hc)
    1. Business enterprises—Computer networks.   2. World Wide Web
(information retrieval system).   I. Samsel, Jon.   II. Title.
HD30.37.W56   1999
658'.054768—dc21   99-37911
                                                             CIP

Printed in Canada

Table of Contents

Foreword
Things Will Never Be the Same!

Dead Ahead invokes an image of businesses moving in their set directions at lighting speed, when suddenly something unforeseen blocks their course and—splat—they come to a screeching halt. This is the perfect metaphor for what the Web will do to many companies, in industries as diverse as steel manufacturing and wine selling. I believe we are at the beginning of a customer revolution that will forever alter the future of buyer-seller interactions.

The age of the empowered customer has arrived. Unprecedented access to information, pricing, availability, suppliers, and delivery options has created a power shift—giving the buyer the prerogative to set the terms of engagement. How companies deal with this newly empowered buyer will make the difference between winning and losing in the new economy.

Let's examine a familiar consumer transaction that most of us can relate to: buying a new car. In my work as a board member at autobytel.com, I have become aware of some interesting data concerning the auto-buying process. Regardless of the efforts of manufacturers and some auto dealers in the automotive industry, buying a new car remains one of the most dreaded experiences a consumer can face. The sales process, designed over decades, has a fairly simple goal: get the customer to pay the maximum price for the vehicle and to drive it home today. Dealers have learned that if you leave the showroom without making a commitment, the likelihood of your returning to finalize the purchase is almost nil. So buyers and sellers have evolved via a Darwinian process; the best prices go to consumers who are battle-ready and are determined to win. While many services over the years have developed to help consumers better understand automobile pricing and the buying process, none have been adopted widely enough to change the game.

In recent conversations with colleagues and acquaintances, I discovered a remarkable trend. Over 90 percent of those asked used the Internet at some point for the car-buying process. Granted, this is somewhat skewed by the Northern California sample, but the usage of online car-buying services like *www.autobytel.com* is growing at such a rapid pace that dealers and manufacturers are beginning to take note. Several of the major dealer groups and a few of the larger manufacturers have announced intentions to use the Web to facilitate marketing of new and used cars on the Internet.

I believe that services such as these, which recognize and empower the consumer, will be the winners. This is great news for consumers. Because of the Web, you can walk into a dealer's showroom with all of the details of your transaction predetermined, have a cup of coffee, and drive away in your new car—happy and still relaxed! Someday soon, the dealer will bring the car to your home or office, and the role of the dealer will be forever changed. The empowering tool in this transformation is the Web, a medium that is putting pressure on existing bricks-and-mortar businesses—dealers, in this case—to offer enough value to continue to have a role in the process.

I find the prospect of this change to be equally gratifying as a consumer and a marketer. As a consumer, I find myself using the Web as my first stop when buying an ever-increasing array of goods and services. The list of things that I buy on the Web has grown steadily over the last twenty-four months, and the number of things I would like to buy is increasing almost daily. I prefer to shop online for things like books, travel, music, toys, computer equipment, consumer electronics, wine, cars, banking services, stock trading, and certain online-only newsletters, to mention a few. In fact, I increasingly get frustrated when things I need to research or would like to buy are not available on the Web. Admittedly, I am an early enthusiast, but I am witnessing this happening to other consumers every day. This shift in preference to do business with companies online happens very quickly for customers. Once they get online and complete their first success-ful transaction, preference follows very rapidly.

From a marketing perspective, I believe the whole process of attracting, informing, selling, and providing service to customers has dramatically changed in this new era. It really doesn't matter whether you're a consumer or a business doing the buying; many of the same forces are driving the transformation of the buying process. Many books have been written over the last few years extolling the virtues of making the customer the focal point and considering the customers' needs as central in every aspect of companies' strategies. Although this customer-centric focus is critical for remaining competitive, an understanding of customer preferences and the nature of the customer relationship has been difficult for companies to obtain and integrate into the strategic process. The Web changes that, too.

As former CEO of Preview Travel, I recall trying to discover how to create a compelling brand and attract and retain leisure-travel customers. During the investigation process we learned that consumers were very frustrated with the pricing of airline tickets and the travel-buying experience in general. They wanted someone to demystify the process and facilitate the transaction "on their terms." For example, one of the key "terms" was being able to plan and transact seven days a week and twenty-four hours a day, which had been impossible because most travel agencies are only open from nine to five, Monday through Friday.

This notion of understanding how the current alternatives were falling short of customer requirements was the basis for the development of our online experience, the branding, the advertis-ing, the customer service, and overall strategic direction of Preview Travel. In the development of this strategy, the consumer's terms were the central focus of the business model evolution. The ability to monitor the Web and analyze consumers' behavior during interaction with the product or any aspect of the site allows for strategic refinement based on real consumer data. And it is faster than ever imaginable. Companies built on this premise of continually monitoring Web customers' preferences and refining the site experience based on those preferences will have a competitive advantage in the future.

For all of us, from online auction pioneer Jerry Kaplan at ONSALE to the early leader in online wine sales, Virtual Vineyards, the process of observing consumer preferences for buying everything from computers at auction to that special bottle of wine has been the driving force for business growth. The commonality in my experiences in building Preview Travel, or as a board member at autobytel.com, ONSALE, or Virtual Vineyards, is clear. These companies are much closer to their customers than any of their "analog" competitors. They are using this knowledge to refine the customer proposition, seemingly on the fly, and that is what has made them successful. This should sound a warning signal to companies large and small; a battle for your customers is raging and your customers are leading the charge. Companies have two choices: to recognize the change of customer preferences and adapt, or to prepare for significant market-share loss and potential business declines. This may seem a bit dramatic, but as customers take control of the process, and technology allows them to explore different ways of doing business, loyalty takes on new meaning. Partnering with customers to meet their needs, on their terms, will define business relationships in the future.

There are numerous stories today of customers changing suppliers because of the ability to interact and transact over the Web. These examples can be found in everything from sophisticated networking equipment to toys, and this will continue as more and more buyers demand alternatives to traditional sales channels and processes. The understanding of this systemic change needs to be internalized by business people at all levels. Whether you're a CEO of a Fortune 500 company or a middle manager in a smaller company, the responsibility to understand the impact of the Web on your company starts with you. If you are reading this and are not yet online or have yet to make that first purchase, you're late! Get wired, buy this book online for someone else like you, and remember—now that the Web is part of our world, things will never be the same.

KENNETH J. ORTON
Summer 1999

Preface

The idea for this book was initially stimulated by my consulting work with high technology companies. As I faced the ongoing challenge of understanding what their customers wanted and developed business, marketing, and product strategies to fit their requirements, it became clear to me that enabling e-business relationships would become strategically imperative for companies across many industries. I believed that this phenomenon would happen first in the business-to-business technology markets and quickly ramp in other markets as well. Our research showed that technology customers had two characteristics that qualified them as early adopters of the Web: They had ready access to Internet technology and liked using it, and they were often adverse to direct vendor-human interaction. Therefore, they were quick to demand that their vendors (my clients) serve their needs via the Internet.

At that point in time, many companies had Web sites that were simply static online brochures. Some companies were experimenting with using the Web as a business vehicle, but actual business-to-business e-commerce was still in its infancy, and many market prognosticators were skeptical about whether the Web would really be taken seriously as a business vehicle.

I remember the actual moment when it struck me that the Web was a cataclysmic force for my business-to-business clients to reckon with. I was conducting a focus group with business-purchase decision-makers—people who had the power to decide what computers would be purchased for their companies. One of the companies told the story of how it had switched its brand loyalty from one well-known vendor (I won't mention the name) to another—Dell. The switch had been made due to one important factor: Dell allowed companies to purchase products and get customer support from the Web. Here we had two leading computer companies, the preference for which was determined by the experience enabled by a Web site.

It was in that focus group when I first realized the Web Effect[SM] phenomenon. I remember thinking that, for a brief period, enabling business relationships via the Web would be a brand differentiator and a tool to build market share for the companies who were early to offer such a presence. Further, I could see that the market would quickly evolve so that enabling e-business relationships would become a "price of entry"—a business requirement to serve customers' future demands. I believed that facing or being blindsided by this phenomenon could make or break companies.

So, my firm, Cognitiative, Inc., had the good fortune to see this Web tidal wave early on. More importantly, we have had the opportunity to work with some of the world's most innovative companies to develop a deeper understanding of customer requirements, help create organizations, and invent business processes for strategically and tactically integrating this new vehicle into highly dynamic business environments.

This book is based on that work. There are many people who have helped me to develop my theories and flesh out the ideas in this book.

I credit Pattie Walters Barco, formerly of Sun Microsystems, for affording my firm the opportunity to become more Web-savvy as we together forged new trails at her company in comprehending and addressing customer requirements.

I thank Jon Samsel for introducing me to the world of book publishing. Without Jon this book would not have been produced. I also thank Jon for his thorough research, his many hours of brainstorming and creating drafts, and his continued enthusiasm for the project.

Thanks to Kathy Stershic, who stepped in and wrote, edited, and refined several portions of this book. Kathy was able to take raw ideas and turn them into interesting prose under intense deadline pressure. Her skill and energy pushed this project into completion.

Thanks to the other team members at Cognitiative, who have contributed to this effort in numerous ways over the last year, including Tara Brown, Kathy Kleinhans, Marcia Lowenstein, and Krim Stephenson.

Thanks to the many Web pioneers who offered their insights about their businesses and their experiences in e-business. These include: Robert Langer, Director, Dell Online, Dell Computer; Chris Sinton, Director, Cisco Connections Online; Anthony Sanchez, Senior Program Manager, 1 to 1 Marketing, Oracle Support Services; Ned Hoyt, President/Founder, iOwn.com; Laurel Scimone Peppino, Communications Manager, iOwn.com; Pamela Roberts, Senior Director, E-Business, Symantec Corporation; Barry Peters, Marketing Director, ONSALE; Chuck Harstad, Vice President of Corporate Marketing, 3M; Jim Radford, Internet Marketing Services Manager, 3M; Tom Panelas, Director of Corporate Communications, Encyclopaedia Britannica; Philip Onigman, Director of Marketing Services, Analytical Divisions, Millipore Corporation; Tom Anderson, Corporate Director of Marketing Communications, Millipore Corporation; Kevin Derella, Franchise Development Manager, 1-800-Flowers; Darrell Ticehurst, President, INSWEB; Deborah Tyroler, Southwest Business Development Manager, International Communications, Inc.; Robert Rodin, President and CEO, Marshall Industries; Dan Marusich, Manager of Internet Communications, Apple Computer; Stuart Wolff, Chairman and CEO, RealSelect, Inc./Realtor.com; Jim Vastyan, Director of Marketing, Primis

Custom Publishing/McGraw-Hill; Aaron Downey, CEO, Roundpeg; Ricardo Garcia Zetina, Director of Marketing and Channels, Centura Software de Mexico; Ruth Ann Feinberg, Manager, Electronic Commerce Division, French Trade Commission; Jim Codrea, Cofounder, Lehigh Valley Safety Shoes; Kennedy Brooks, Executive Vice President, Global Planning and Development, NETEQ Corporation; Gilma Guevarra, Marketing Programs Manager, Vision Software; Phil Gibson, Director of Interactive Marketing, National Semiconductor; Stephanie Race, Practice Director, Oracle Consulting Services; and David Perry, CEO and Founder, Chemdex, Inc.

Thanks to the hundreds of people who have allowed Cognitiative to query, prod, and challenge them in our Pulse of the Customer[SM] research. It is their attitudes, preferences, and enthusiasm that have validated over and over again how critical the Web has become in this age of the empowered customer.

And finally, enormous thanks to Ken Orton for his undying energy in helping form the ideas for this book. His willingness to discuss concepts, test theories, and edit chapters has been critical to this project. Without his support, this book would not have been written.

LAURIE WINDHAM
Summer 1999

The Inevitability of the Web as a Business Vehicle: Requirements to Adapt to the New Rules of Doing Business

"The Web presents a new series of challenges that few organizations are prepared to deal with. For a company like Dell—which is perceived as a first mover in the Internet space—we constantly struggle with moving our strategic vision forward. What to do next becomes a quarterly concern. We're in uncharted waters, and there's no one else to learn from."

—Robert Langer, Director, Dell Online

The Internet is no longer a phenomenon of the future. It has arrived and is dead ahead in the road to continued success—for many businesses. In an incredibly short period of time, the Web has become a critical vehicle through which to conduct business and build productive relationships with all constituents in the market.

The rapid emergence of the Web as a strategic business vehicle has created a significant dilemma for many companies. We now realize that the Web is more than a function of marketing— it's a process, a tool, a medium, and an experience that truly represents a new way of doing business. Furthermore, it is fast becoming the preferred information and commerce channel of the new economy, a fact that is forcing companies to look beyond their traditional business processes. The old rules about sales, marketing, distribution, and customer support are becoming irrelevant.

Adopting the Web as a key business vehicle presents some very difficult challenges because it strikes at the operational foundation on which many companies are built. Managers are being asked to make decisions today that will have a profound impact on the way they market, sell, fulfill, and support their customers for many years to come. The level of change required to respond to market pressures is truly pervasive for most companies. The dilemma is especially acute for established organizations that now enjoy success in the offline world.

Businesses are at a critical crossroads where they must decide what the Web really means to them. As business leaders grapple with how they intend to migrate from traditional business processes to Internet-enabled or assisted business models, they inevitably face both danger and opportunity. The action they take—either embracing or rejecting the Web—will have a profound impact on the future of their organizations. Business leaders need to understand that there is no doubt about whether the Web will affect their businesses, only about when this communication medium will reach the point where it cannot be ignored.

Many businesses have dealt with this change head on—hiring new types of employees, retraining existing staff, revamping information technology (IT) departments, retooling content publishing practices, getting to know their customers better, and taking a hard look at current business strategies to make sure they are in sync with the economy of the new millennium. Some companies are succeeding. Other companies are in turmoil.

Unfortunately, too many businesses are looking at the Internet as merely a facilitator of e-commerce or an inexpensive way to beef up customer support. They are not really integrating the Web into their entire business operations. Not only can the Internet help streamline a company's internal operations, it can be harnessed to increase sales, improve customer support, build brand awareness, and drive new business.

Business leaders must make tough choices when deciding how to incorporate the Internet into the business process. The strength of your future market position will largely depend on how you manage the transition from your present organizational processes to a model that embraces the Web as a strategic business tool.

How Did This All Happen So Quickly?

Many business managers ask themselves a key question—is the rush to the Web a passing fad or a permanent fixture in the new millennium? How did this happen so fast, and how do we know that it's a permanent business reality? It's helpful to understand the sequence of activity that has brought us to where we are today, and to explain why the Internet is here to stay—a new permanent reality that must be addressed.

Many factors helped fuel the rapid growth of the Internet. Through the convergence of networking and browser and communications technology innovation, the Web became a technical possibility. Technically savvy users quickly became demanders, which helped spur content development and functionality advances. Corporate networks delivered Web access to desktops across the enterprise. Online service providers lured consumer audiences online in record numbers. Ready access to capital created an entrepreneurial climate where hundreds of new Web-related business ventures flourished.

The Internet's growing impact on business is something we refer to as the Web Effect[SM], a precept that loosely plays on Edward Lorenz's chaos theory principle known as the Butterfly Effect.[1] The Butterfly Effect has become a popular metaphor for describing the chaos theory, the notion that the flapping of a butterfly's wings in China can send ripples of effects throughout larger and more complex systems, causing, say, a hurricane in Florida.

Following this analogy, the Web is a true "phenomenon" that is impacting businesses worldwide. The "complex system" being impacted by the Web is our global economy. Much like the ripples in a pond, which originate at a center point and then move outward, the Web affects businesses in ways that cannot be entirely predicted, and that will continue to impact organizations in this unsettling way for many years to come.

The ripples in the Web Effect are illustrated in figure 1.1. The Web Effect begins with access. In the relatively short time frame since the Web has been in existence, we have observed that people with access to the Web—who perform work and personal activities there—quickly develop a preference for the Web as a vehicle for many business and leisure tasks.

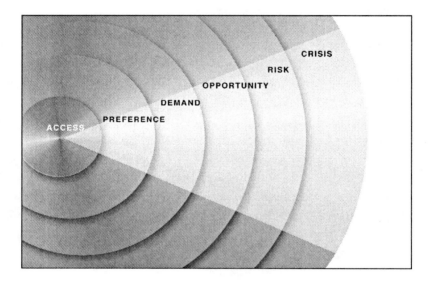

This pattern is very evident when studying early adopters of electronic communications, such as IT professionals. We learned that nearly all IT professionals now indicate that the Web is critical to their job functions. They rely on the Web throughout the business day for vital communications about bugs, patches, user group communication, new product information, pricing, and competitive product reviews. Most IT professionals will say that they can no longer perform their jobs without Web access.

IT professionals were early to feel the Web Effect. They were uniquely positioned to have access to the required technology, to understand how to use it—and thus to not be afraid of it. The vendors with whom they interacted, such as representatives from computer hardware and software companies, realized the need to offer core business functions and content online. As a result—through the Web—IT professionals had access to functionality that was highly relevant to their job success. This access quickly led to preference.

Companies that could address the IT industry's preference for Web-enabled business relationships had an extreme advantage over companies that could not. In fact, in Cognitiative's research studies from 1997 through 1999, we found that IT professionals were not only influenced, but were more likely to do business with vendors whose "Web presence" was analogous with their business needs. Today, this preference continues to gain momentum.

Consumer access to the Internet evolved differently than access in the business arena, due to the efforts of early service providers America Online (AOL), Prodigy, and CompuServe. While these companies had offered proprietary online subscription services for some time, their services really took off (or died) when access to the Web became possible via these online relationships. Intensive marketing efforts—especially from AOL—resulted in providing millions of consumers with easy access to the Web. This was a critical step in transforming the consumer into a much savvier online citizen who preferred the Web to other means of communicating.

While the Web Effect has had initial impact on those companies and households that had early access, the proliferation of Web availability throughout companies, educational institutions, and homes has led to wide-scale access. This access is creating preference to do business and conduct relationships on the Web in every market in our global economy.

"Clearly, the Internet is changing the way business is conducted," says Stuart Wolff, CEO of RealSelect. "It's starting to impact every vertical market there is—real estate, automobiles, books, and nearly every retail segment. It's impacting the supply side, it's impacting the marketing side, and every other way that business is being conducted."

The effect is that the Internet is no longer regarded as an "optional" channel. Business and individual customers now depend on the Internet for finding information, purchasing products, seeking services, and communicating—it has become indispensable for getting things done. The Web, in short, has propagated a systemic change in the way people consume—a remarkable transformation in customer attitudes and behavior.

As individual and business customers develop a preference for using the Web, they are now demanding that businesses service them online. Hundreds of hours of focus groups have shown us that online users not only prefer to do business, interact, and transact online, they are demanding that companies address these needs.

And so, this Web Effect is forcing companies to develop a Web strategy. It is not a flash-in-the-pan phenomenon. Web access and preference are now critical fibers in the fabric of our economy. Customers demand that businesses meet their needs via the Web. And the Web customer is savvier than any customer we've seen before.

The Age of the Empowered Customer

The net result of the Web Effect is that it has created an empowered customer. By providing information regarding many products, and by allowing easy access to many providers of products, the Internet has put the customer in an unprecedented position of control. The Internet is an empowerment tool, providing customers with myriad options they never had before—countless brands to choose from, searchable databases, unique personalization features, numerous shipping options, built-to-order merchandise, instant access/downloads of electronic content, closeout items, items up for auction—the list goes on.

Customers are smarter and more demanding than ever, and the Web is a tool that enables them to conduct sophisticated and extensive comparison shopping. Suspects, prospects, and customers have access to a wealth of information from many companies when they make their buying decisions.

As a result, control of the transaction has shifted from the seller to the buyer, from the vendor to the customer. When you shift control to an online user, it becomes very difficult to take that control away from them later on. It actually becomes more than a demand—the Web becomes a prerequisite to doing business with a company.

"Building relationships with our customers and suppliers is crucial to our business model," remarks David Perry, founder and CEO of Chemdex Corporation, a company that aggregates the process of buying and selling life science products via the Web. "It's all about solving problems. If we can operate a business that solves problems for our customers (broadly defined as buyers and sellers), then we will be successful. Our goal is to figure out what their problems are, get them to communicate those to us, go solve them, and communicate back that we've solved them. If we can do that, then we've built both a relationship and a successful business."[2]

Ken Orton, former president and CEO of Preview Travel, one of the top online travel providers in the world, explains: "We are coming upon an age of a new kind of consumer, one with unprecedented access to product and service information. When it is time to transact, the customer is a completely different kind of buyer. The tool that has enabled this sea change is the Web."

Opportunity or Risk?

Is the Web an opportunity or a risk? The answer is both. Companies that look at the Web as an opportunity to improve customer service, streamline accounting and financial practices, and better meet the information and purchasing needs of its customers and partners will be in a much better position to survive in the networked economy.

But realizing that an opportunity exists is only a small, first step. There are many companies that recognize a window of opportunity but will not be aggressive enough to make the changes necessary to maximize the opportunity. Even after the opportunity is recognized, success or failure will depend on how truly committed a company is to addressing the demands of Web-savvy customers.

The real risk to businesses is this: By being slow to react, you open the door for customer defection to rivals who are able to meet customer needs in an electronic marketplace. By not responding rapidly enough to accommodate the changing needs of customers, businesses pave the way for customer dissatisfaction.

What's holding companies back? The most obvious concern is that any operational upheaval or change in business procedure may adversely affect profitability—and more implicitly, negatively impact business relationships with both partners and customers. These concerns are well founded. The consequence of inaction, however, is far more grave than that of the proactive decisions you make today about what role the Web should play in your business. And, timing of market entry is critical to success.

The Importance of Timing: First In or Forced In?

Some companies were early to embrace the Web as a strategic business vehicle. They saw the Internet coming, and they took action to meet the Web challenge head on. These "first in" businesses recognized the Web as a strategic business opportunity, and their proactive decisions helped propel many of them to early leadership in their markets. Companies who are slow to respond—those who are "forced in"—are put into the unenviable position of having to defend their "late to market" Web strategies rather than focusing on the virtues of their brands. It's a defensive position, it's not terribly flattering to the corporate image, and it's risky—once customer preference and loyalty is lost, they can be both difficult and expensive to win back.

"A company that isn't on the Web over the next year or so will have very little hope of ever catching up, because it takes a long time for companies to put in place the organizational and processing procedures," claims Darrell Ticehurst, president of InsWeb, the Web's leading information aggregator for helping consumers do online comparison shopping for insurance. "We're still encountering companies that are having trouble with their internal electronic commerce procedures. Even companies who jumped in early—back in 1995—need to work through the enormous inertia associated with a bureaucracy that's used to handling things in a certain way."[3]

	PROS	CONS
First In	Lock in market position & customer loyalty	Expensive market development
Forced In	Market demand developed	Market position and loyalty taken

The significance of being "first in" should not be understated. Early online innovators have gained a psychological edge, if not a clear-cut business advantage. Technology-wise, they have a powerful grasp of what it takes to deliver an advanced online experience combined with broad, innovative content offerings.

Many "first in" firms are also able to attract the best talent—employees in the online world want to work for companies that are perceived as technological leaders. Companies positioned for rapid growth, which can offer employees competitive salaries and profit participation, have a big advantage over traditional firms that cannot make similar offerings to new hires. But perhaps the most significant advantage for "first in" businesses is their ability to create real barriers to competitor entry by locking down multiyear business alliances with popular online destination sites or portals such as Excite, Lycos, Go Network, Yahoo!

etc., making it much harder for competitors to enter the same online space.

Companies forced onto the Web are often established corporations entrenched in time-honored business processes that feel compelled to develop a Web strategy because of technology innovations, competitive pressures, or customer demands—not because they are innovators. Size is no protector. In fact, the bigger these firms are, the more they stand to lose. Getting a big company to change the way it does business is extremely difficult.

Many businesses will face an uphill battle when they attempt to alter the status quo. And they are often not prepared to make the necessary resource commitments to be successful. J. Neil Weintraut, a partner at 21st Century Internet Partners, a venture capital firm specializing in technology companies, sums up the battle: "Large corporations are approaching the Web with too low a level of commitment. BDCs [Big Dumb Companies] are encumbered with initiatives based on old-world models."[4]

"Forced in" companies are especially dependent on aggressive and enthusiastic support for change from upper-level management. In fact, there won't be any movement toward a Web-centric business strategy without bold leadership. Web-savvy management has to be in place and willing to back the painful choices that will be necessary to integrate Internet transactions into already existing practices.

Dell Computer, for example, was one of a few companies to have seen the Web Effect coming far in advance of any crisis— and it crafted a unique online value proposition for its customers to gain an edge on its competitors. Dell initiated a cross-functional Internet strategy managed by a central Web division when the medium was still in its infancy. The company figured out how to utilize the Web to enhance its bottom line by transferring sales to a lower cost channel—from direct sales via telephone to interactive relationships via the Web. This Web strategy was a natural extension of Dell's existing direct-marketing model, whereby it sold exclusively through direct field or telesales representatives rather than through two-tier distribution, as was the norm . among its competitors.

In 1997 Dell introduced customized Web sites for its large and midsize customers—a program called Premier Pages. Premier Pages are customized Web sites that can be set up quickly to meet specific customer business requirements. With Premier Pages, a company can have its own Web page at the Dell Web site that contains purchasing procedures—such as approved computer configurations, negotiated prices, and purchase authority limits—unique to the business relationship. This cuts order times from several weeks to several days, saving both parties money. Plus, it helps decrease order errors. These customized sites also include tools to help companies track their Dell computers by serial number, obtain shipment status, and integrate purchase into legacy databases to help streamline the entire ordering process.

Dell's Premier Pages have effectively created a customized version of *www.dell.com* for each customer. In early 1999, there were more than 8,500 Premier Pages for customers around the world. Premier Pages allow participating companies to establish standard configurations for ordering desktops, laptops, and servers—and those standard configurations are viewable on a company-specific version of the Dell Premier Page. The service takes into account volume commitments, pricing agreements, employee purchasing options, and discount levels—providing companies with an efficient asset-management capability. Premier Pages are the window into Dell for that customer relationship.

Dell's move stimulated its competitors to react defensively. Compaq introduced a wave of Web strategies designed to accommodate user demands while pacifying its distribution channels. IBM began offering customers the option to build to order. Apple Computer opened the Apple Store to offer similar online ordering capabilities. In spite of these efforts, these "forced in" companies lost market share to Dell. In fact, numerous technology customers we surveyed in 1998 said they switched brands from Compaq to Dell for the sole reason that Dell enabled them to order products and get customer support online. Many respondents commented that "Dell makes it easier for companies to do business."

According to a January 1999 report by Dataquest, Compaq continued to lead the worldwide PC industry with a 13.1 percent market share in 1998, while Dell's market share grew 65 percent to 5.5 percent in 1998. Dell also posted the strongest growth increase in the United States market, rising 60.9 percent to a 12.2 percent market share behind Compaq's 16.1 percent share.[5] And according to quarterly ranking by Technology Business Research, Dell Computer is now the overall leader in enterprise computing sales, surpassing Sun Microsystems and Compaq Computer respectively.[6] Only time will tell whether the amount of ground these competitors lost to Dell can be regained.

View from the Bottom Line

Of course, looking at the impact of the Web on the top line is only one metric of the Web Effect. Another key imperative to resolve the Web dilemma is the bottom line. Over time, the operational savings that result from effective use of Web technology throughout the enterprise will dramatically impact companies' costs of doing business and profitability.

Cisco Systems is an outstanding example of a "first in" company that has learned how to make its Web presence a critical component of its competitiveness, not only because of customer preference, but because of gross margin improvement due to operational efficiencies.

Cisco Systems launched its Web initiative, Cisco Connection Online (CCO), in 1993 at a cost of about $3 million. Today, the firm continues its quest to "Webify" its global network operations, saving Cisco millions of dollars while simultaneously increasing customer satisfaction. Cisco's results are impressive. By automating the ordering process, CCO has shaved inaccurate orders down to less than one percent. They've reduced by roughly 40 percent the amount of time customer service reps spend on taking and inputting orders—freeing them up to focus on better service and relationship building. The company generates over 70 percent of its total annual revenue over the Web; its goal for 1999 is 80 percent. CCO has enabled the firm to serve over 1,200 business entities—businesses that now order Cisco products exclusively online. All told, including savings harvested from manufacturing, the Internet is saving Cisco about $500 million a year and helping preserve its 32 percent operating margins.

"We've seen a huge financial impact in terms of cost savings," says Chris Sinton, Director, Cisco Connection. "In 1999 alone, we'll save about half a billion dollars in the areas of commerce, supply chain, and employee self-service. But one of the most exciting indicators of our success online is in customer relations. Customer satisfaction has risen from 3.4, on a 1 to 5 scale, to 4.32. Our customers and partners are choosing to use the Internet to conduct business, and they're more satisfied in doing business that way. We certainly haven't shut off our phones or pulled the plugs on the fax machine, but there is inherent value in twenty-four/seven worldwide access. It's a pretty strong value proposition for someone considering doing business with us."[7]

Clearly, the Web has helped Cisco's profitability. And by doing so, it has made it more competitive. Not only does Cisco win new customers who prefer doing business via the Web but, more importantly, the resulting profit-margin improvement puts Cisco in a position to compete through increased technology investments, market expansion, or decreased product prices. The more profitable company is always the most significant competitor in the long run.

Cisco is not the only company using electronic commerce to realize significant cost savings and increased sales opportunities. There is a growing array of examples. Idaho-based Boise Cascade, the $2 billion office products wholesaler and business-to-business process manager for office products procurement, is a prominent case in point.

Boise Cascade (*www.bcop.com*) was a "first in" in its marketplace—in early 1997 it placed its entire product catalog of ten thousand–plus items on the Web. The cost? Since many of its customers did not have ready access to the Web in the workplace at that time, the company projected that only a small percentage of them would order from the site during the first year of operations. And they were right—only about 5 percent of them did. But after only six months of operation, the Boise Cascade site paid for itself—saving the company more than $1 million in operating expenses and increasing the company's overall cost savings by 20 percent. By year-end 1998, nearly one in ten Boise Cascade customers regularly purchased office products from its Web site— and Boise estimates that customers transacting online have saved over 30 percent in processing costs alone.

The New Rules of Business

Why aren't companies moving faster to offer Web sites that enable commerce, customer service, marketing assistance, or distribution support? Our research shows that real operational issues stand in the way of progress. We believe that capturing opportunities and mitigating risks require companies to operate according to a new set of rules: the Web Rules of Business. Being able to adapt well to the Web Rules of Business is key to the long-term survival of many companies. To be competitive, companies need to understand the new rules and overcome the barriers to change.

These six Web rules are derived from thousands of hours of Cognitiative's Pulse of the Customer^{SM} research, from our work helping a variety of companies develop Web business strategies, and from dealing with the internal issues that emerge when companies go through a major change in how they do business. The remainder of this book is devoted to discussing these rules and topics in greater detail.

In this chapter we've discussed the inevitability of the Web as a business vehicle. In chapter 2, we explore the first key rule: Know what your market requires. Our research has shown that the empowered customer on the Web has common demands for what we call a Whole Experience^{SM}. But, how to address those demands in a fulfilling and differentiated way requires a deep understanding of your customers.

Do you know what your customers really want in terms of e-commerce? What are your competitors providing? The basic steps to defining customer requirements are the same in the offline and online worlds: survey the market landscape; talk to your target users/customers; determine the needs of prospects; find out what partners need to support the relationship; test the usability of the site experience; and track user satisfaction.

Companies have a lot to learn about what the market wants before they can make their Web sites more productive and engaging to the people who use them day after day. Armed with this critical research data, companies can better understand why people come to their site, what actions they take when they are there, and where those users are in the Consumption Cycle[SM]. We use the phrase "consumption cycle" to explain the integration of marketing, sales, and customer-usage activities (shopping, buying, receiving, consuming) into one cohesive Web site. This knowledge can then be used to develop a proactive Web site strategy that satisfies user needs.

Resolving conflict with existing business strategies is the topic of chapter 3. Strategy conflict is by far the most critical barrier to doing business on the Internet. It can run the whole gamut from pricing to sales and distribution strategy to customer-relationship management. A key strategy issue is how best to transition from legacy processes to Web-enabled processes without breaking the existing business model. For most companies, the business strategy conflict lies in how they sell. Channel conflict issues are being fueled by companies looking for ways to go around wholesalers and reach their customers directly. The Web presents an opportunity for companies to reexamine how they buy and sell goods. Slow response to sales channel issues has given rise to online upstarts such as Amazon.com, eToys, and Chemdex—all companies that have figured out how to utilize the Web as an optimal sales and supply chain tool.

Establishing and sustaining brand loyalty is the focus of chapter 4. The Web presents some unique and some not-so-unique challenges in establishing and building a brand. For companies that have invested heavily in building brand equity in the analog world, the Web presents a perplexing problem—how to translate the brand promise in this new digital world. How can a Web site attract, build, and sustain brand preference in the absence of human interface and tactile contact? Many companies have tried to deliver on their brand promise on the Web. Some have succeeded and some have failed. This challenge is not trivial—and it is vital to long-term brand survival.

In chapter 5, we look at executive leadership, organizational structures, skill sets, and funding models for success on the Web. When introducing Web commerce to an organization, executive managers need to remember that all employees will eventually be affected, even if their current job descriptions do not require them to have these Web-oriented skills. These new skills are not limited to duties such as programming, Web design, or information management. An Internet-ready employee must know how the Internet impacts all segments of the workplace. This means everybody—information technologists, marketing managers, customer support representatives, and even salespeople—will need to know how to contribute, if they are empowered to do so. It also means that businesses must educate their employees to work towards a participatory Web effort.

There are other organizational issues to be considered, such as budgeting and funding. If only one department within a company is responsible for the Web budget, the company may not be allocating enough resources to truly make the Internet a strategic business vehicle for the entire organization. A successful Whole Experience Web presence requires that the various functional areas within a company be aligned and motivated to work together as one cohesive machine.

Chapter 6 focuses on today's businesses' need to make intelligent, long-term decisions about investing in the core technology infrastructure that will enable Whole Experiences for their customers. This involves a broad range of functionality—from content publishing and databases to security and report generation. Companies that do not commit adequate resources to develop an effective site that satisfies customer needs are putting themselves at a substantial disadvantage. Solutions include investments in technologies that enable dynamic, personalized content and content creation throughout the organization.

In chapter 7 we focus on the barriers that prevent the extension of your Web presence around the world. These issues include not only language and cultural differences, but legal, tax, and technology infrastructure as well.

Chapter 8 is a corporate road map—a series of checklists and questions—designed to help readers put the ideas in this book into practice. It's a transition guide and analysis tool for planning, implementing, evaluating, and upgrading your corporate Web site strategy.

Summary

Nearly every major company operates a Web site today. But those Web sites are in various states of effectiveness—ranging from online brochures to fully functional business vehicles. The pace at which Web sites must evolve to become more potent business vehicles is largely gated by specific markets' access to Web, the rate of Web-preference development, and competitors' strategies. One thing is clear, however—it's happening more quickly than we ever imagined.

In late 1998 we conducted a series of focus groups comprised of business decision-makers from major U.S. metropolitan areas. Regardless of company size or industry type, all the respondents indicated that within twelve months their companies' Web presence would become a strategic business vehicle, if they were not already there. And they believed that their companies' Web sites were key to their competitiveness in their markets.[8]

The Web has become a new point of contact between companies and their constituents. The company Web site is now a vital link in the business chain, surpassing all reasonable expectations to become the medium of choice for conducting electronic commerce, exchanging information, and servicing needs. In fact, once business customers and consumers use the Web to meet their needs, it is virtually impossible for them to return to the old way of doing things—they are hooked. As we find ourselves squarely in this new era, where the Web has become a primary point of contact for customers, the Web site bears the responsibility of simplifying business processes—whether that process is buying, selling, receiving, consuming, or servicing a deliverable commodity.

Businesses must recognize that the Web is a revolution, not an evolution. The Web dilemma is being created by customers' demands and market pressures. To remain competitive, businesses must recognize this power shift and begin to place the Web in the mainstream of their business strategies.

It is becoming pretty apparent that for businesses to succeed in the new economy, Web-related issues need to be addressed quickly, efficiently, and at the highest levels within an organization. How should companies deal with customer preference? How should they deal with the dynamics of the empowered consumer? How should they deal with the "access plus preference" dynamic that's going on in the business-to-business and consumer markets?

"Business leaders need to look at the spaces they're in and decide how important the Web is going to be to their businesses in the next three years, and then they have to act now," says Kenneth J. Orton, former CEO of Preview Travel.

Today's businesses must meet the dead-ahead challenges presented by the Web straight on. There will be two basic kinds of organizations left after the Web dilemma is resolved—those who embraced the Web with determination, and those who wish they had.

Chapter Two

Comprehend and Facilitate the Consumption Behavior of Your Market

"We believe in the power of the informed customer."

—Ned Hoyt, Cofounder and CEO, iOwn.com

The Internet has introduced and made possible a new mode of consumer behavior. People are more informed and have better information—they are more empowered. Just as the Web has enabled a new mode of consumer behavior, so too has it created a need for vendors to take a fresh look at what their markets demand so as to understand and facilitate this new behavior.

The first new rule of business requires that companies comprehend and facilitate the consumption behaviors of their market. They must invest in discovering their customers' wants and needs regarding the Web and gain a deeper understanding of who these people are and why they are online. And they must learn how to stimulate and maintain the desired customer behavior via the Web site.

Fundamentally, how is the vendor/customer relationship different in the Web world? There are several basic differences. Customers become more autonomous and have less direct contact with the company when the Web becomes *the* way they experience a company. In this nonpersonal mode of interaction, developing trust is more critical than ever before. How well the site delivers a positive and productive experience is the stuff of which trust is built.

"On the Internet, we do customer service differently," says Tony Levitan, president of E-greetings Network. "As cybermerchants, we must build strong customer relationships without personal contact. The customer needs to know the person behind the site."[1]

The challenge for business leaders is to create a trusting online environment—a two-way relationship that leverages the company brand, builds loyalty, and drives customers through each phase of the Consumption Cycle. Customer loyalty in the online world is about delivering what you promise—namely, a satisfying experience. The sum total of all the user's experience on a Web site is what builds trust, and ultimately, preferences.

Ned Hoyt, cofounder and CEO of iOwn.com (formerly HomeShark, Inc.), an online provider of discounted mortgages and home-buying advice, says, "A Web site should improve the consumer experience by offering a secure environment that is easy to use."[2]

An example of a highly diverse company that has recognized the need to design its Web strategy from the customer perspective is 3M. When 3M first launched its online presence, each of its various divisions created its own Web page, designed around its own products or product groups. The company's new customer-centric Web strategy is comprised of ten customer centers and one 3M corporate site. "Customer centers are the way our customers view 3M via the Web," says Chuck Harstad, vice president of corporate marketing, 3M. "The problem with rolling out our Web site the old way is that we ended up with a myriad of sites that were difficult to navigate and left the customer fairly confused. Some of our customers said they might defect to a competitor if we didn't get our act together, so we made a serious effort to listen to them and find ways we could improve our site. We took an outside-in versus an inside-out perspective and said,

'If we were a customer, how would we view 3M?' I think we had to go through this learning process to realize our Web effort wasn't as good as it could be. We are now committed, more than ever, to satisfying our customers."[3]

For some companies it is easier to build customer relationships in a Web world than in the offline world, especially for companies who have traditionally relied on middlemen to get products to target customers. For these companies, it may be that the first time that they have actually had ongoing, direct contact with customers is on the Web. The Web offers a wonderful opportunity to get to know customer needs, behaviors, and preferences.

For companies that have always fostered a direct relationship with their customers, creating a Web experience that substitutes, improves upon, and complements the direct relationship is a significant hurdle. But as we progress through this new era, where the Web site is a primary point of contact for customers—an environment that bears the responsibility of simplifying entire business processes—many companies are being forced to address this challenge.

Whatever the traditional relationship structure between vendors and customers, in the Web world delivering on an enduring value proposition, improving customer relationships, and building brand loyalty are a different beast. Web relationships with customers only last as long as companies work to preserve and improve customers' site experiences. It's the duty of businesses to deliver what customers want, when they want it. Customer preference is experience-dependent, and empowered customers are not prone to be as loyal to any single brand. They have a different set of expectations—different rules for how they want to be treated.

Demands of the Empowered Customer

What constitutes a fulfilling experience that causes customers to come back repeatedly? While approaches vary widely, successful Web strategies are based on four basic principles—the "demands of the empowered customer." These are guidelines that companies should follow to ensure that they are addressing the basic expectations of target customers, both businesses and individuals.

"GIVE ME WHAT I NEED WHEN I NEED IT."

Wherever they are in a cycle of consuming—learning, shopping, buying, using—customers want companies to anticipate and offer what they need in one cohesive experience. But many companies don't think about all the actions their prospects and customers take in one logical continuum, because in the analog world these activities are addressed by distinctly different departments. Companies that integrate marketing, sales, fulfillment, and customer service departments' activities into one integrated Web system have a distinct advantage, because the site—in absence of human contact—essentially "pulls" people through the logical sequence of consuming, which we call the Consumption Cycle.

"DON'T WASTE MY TIME."

Contrary to some popular opinions, most of today's Web users don't "surf." They are time deprived and usually come to the site with a specific purpose in mind. This is true of both business and individual consumers.

Business-to-business Web sites must enable users to perform their jobs better. Business customers want Web sites to empower them to do the things they need to do. To them, visiting Web sites is about getting a job done—not cruising.

One of the top benefits to using the Internet in business is that it can increase productivity. Productive Web sites have a depth of content (addressing all visitors' needs) and a breadth of content (the full range of things visitors might want to do). They are destinations where users can go to get practical content— things like pricing, product specifications, quick and easy access to technical support, and comparative analysis.

At home, individual customers are also deprived of time. In fact, a key reason they are using the Web is *because* they are time deprived. These days, few people have the luxury of leisure time. While "productivity" at home may require different specific Web site features and functions, the desire to be productive is as important to the home user as to the business user.

Another important consideration is where a visitor is in her stage of purchase decision or consumption. What is productive to a prospect is different than what is productive to a customer. A prospect's idea of Web productivity is a place where he can go to get purchase information, pricing, product specifications, comparative analysis, and basic company data. A customer's idea of Web productivity is a site that provides quick and easy access to technical support, tracking of orders, product updates, chat rooms, frequently asked questions (FAQs), and the like.

Many online merchants fail to deliver on their productivity promise. Finding out if a company can ship in time for delivery on a certain day, for example, is a service few commerce sites offer at the present time. Real-time inventory status—a feature that lets consumers know which items are in stock prior to placing an online order—is another key feature missing from many sites. Customers are turned off when they receive an e-mail notice, days after their initial purchase, stating that a particular item they ordered is on back order. Not only is this maddening for the consumer and a complete waste of time, but it is an unacceptable business practice.

"GIVE ME MEANINGFUL CONTENT, NOT FLUFF."

Customers want engaging content—not propaganda. The one thing today's Web visitor will not tolerate is unwanted marketing material "pushed on them" over the Web. Users will "click away" when they sense they are being "sold." To get marketing messages across in an effective way, companies need to integrate them throughout the site's content so that the users receive and interact with the messages on their own terms. The content must hold their attention, empower them, and cause them to want to come back. This is engagement—and it's not an easy technique to master.

"DON'T EXPLOIT ME."

People are increasingly suspicious of how information will be used for marketing. That's because some companies are misusing and abusing information gathered from online commerce by sending unsolicited junk mail, known as spam, and by selling the information to third parties. Companies who misuse information are running the risk of losing many customers who strongly resent this type of exploitation. And be advised, many times customers can figure out who sold their names by using different spellings and versions of their names to trap the exploiter and cease the relationship.

Proper business etiquette is really just common sense. Companies should give users a choice as to whether or not they want to be subjected to marketing promotions that rely on registration data, and they should deliver on their registration promises. No tricks, gimmicks, or deception.

People are willing to register, if they must, to get access to job or task critical data. But they draw the line when sites ask for personal information—such as income, age, education, and home address—that is irrelevant to the task at hand. For a successful registration, trust must be earned and user rights must be respected.

There is also the issue of credit card security when ordering products and services online. People remain concerned about revealing their credit card information over the Internet, although they are less concerned than they used to be. Encryption technology and strong corporate Web purchasing policies have helped to raise consumer confidence levels.

"Addressing security concerns is an educational process," says Robert Olson, cofounder of Virtual Vineyards. "We have a funny story about a customer who didn't feel comfortable sending his credit card information through an encrypted online transaction. So, from his car, he called from his cellular phone and placed his order. Figure that one out!"[4]

Clearly, educating customers about what and when something is secure is key to overcoming concerns about security.

The Whole Experience

When you factor the demands of the empowered customer together, the result is that people want a "whole experience" that is based on their interpretation of the rules. What is a Whole Experience? It extends beyond the notion of "whole product," an idea that Theodore Levitt describes in his book, *The Marketing Imagination*.[5] Levitt states that a gap exists between the marketing promise made to the customer (the value proposition) and the ability of a shipped product to fulfill that promise. To bridge that gap, Levitt says that manufacturers must add value to the product by providing services and ancillary products to the offering to create a whole product.

Playing on that concept, a Whole Experience Web site integrates marketing, sales, and customer-usage activities; as seen in figure 2.1, it serves all aspects of the Consumption Cycle—shopping, buying, receiving, and consuming—in one cohesive Web site. It puts the user in the center of the universe, anticipating, stimulating, and facilitating her behavior. It fulfills the promise of the company's value proposition by satisfying user needs.

THE ROLE OF THE WEB SITE MAPPED TO THE CONSUMPTION CYCLESM

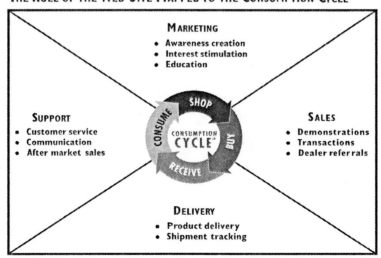

While the steps in the Consumption Cycle are traditional, the sequence and lines of demarcation between them blur when the Web is the vehicle of facilitation. This means that the deployment

required to support the Consumption Cycle cannot follow the traditional org-chart/silo-centric model (vertical, delineated business units functioning independently of one other). Deploying a Whole Experience via the Web requires that the stakeholders integrate their efforts and the site be designed to provide the user with a cohesive, integrated experience.

The Whole Experience concept impacts all elements of doing business: marketing, sales, fulfillment, and customer service.

MARKETING

The emergence of the Web as the primary business vehicle has significant implications for the marketing department. The traditional roles of marketing—raising awareness, stimulating interest, educating, and encouraging product trial—persist as key roles in the Whole Experience Web site. But, the challenges of successfully pulling people through the Consumption Cycle are different.

The Internet is forcing us reconsider what we currently know about marketing—in several realms. While the end goal is the same, fundamentally, the marketing challenge is different in three key areas: In a Web world, you have no control of who comes to the site and when they do so. Therefore, targeting for messages, offers, and programs is radically different. Secondly, when the Web is the primary marketing vehicle, it becomes *the* focal point for establishing and maintaining brand identity. How well the Web experience meets the needs and expectations of visitors plays a crucial role in establishing and maintaining brand loyalty. Thirdly, the Web enables a sophisticated dialogue between vendors and their customers. When well executed, the Web site can yield information that is critical to meeting the ongoing and future needs of the customer. These three fundamental changes enabled by the Web grossly impact strategic and tactical marketing.

Every first-time visitor to a Web site initially sees the same thing. He can also come to the site whenever he chooses. The first formidable task that the Web puts in front of us is how to adapt our business practices to a marketing vehicle that is "omnipresent." Since companies don't have control over who visits their Web site and when, they don't know if their online visitors are shopping, looking for support, or simply browsing.

The process that customers go through to make a purchase decision in the online versus the offline worlds are very much the same. Consumers still have to become aware of a need for something before they can consider buying it. Once an item or service becomes a purchase option, the prospect has to seriously evaluate it before she decides to buy it. Once an item has been purchased, a relationship between company and customer commences. How that relationship proceeds and endures, however, is experience dependent.

Fostering positive experiences via the Web is a complex challenge. A site should not only pull prospects and consumers through the Consumption Cycle, it should also encourage them to do something. If you zoom in on the shopping part of the equation, a Web site should help transform an online visitor from being "mildly aware" to "somewhat interested" to "truly considering" to "really evaluating whether to buy" to "making a decision." That's a huge responsibility to place on a medium devoid of human interaction.

This concept of the Web being an "on-demand channel" is very different from the time-phased, targeted marketing campaigns deployed in the analog world. Until the advent of the Web, marketing vehicles were selected based on target audiences. Ad insertions were selected based on reader profiles; direct mail was sent to users with known demographic attributes. But, by its very nature, access to a Web site is undifferentiated. A site has to be able to target itself to the user. With the Web, targeting has to be done on the fly. This requires advanced underlying technology to adapt the users' experience, based on past and current behavior demonstrated on the Web site. (We will examine these technologies in chapter 6.) It also requires creating content that's dynamic and compelling for specific target segments.

The second formidable task concerning Web marketing is that for the first time, the user's online experience shapes the impression of the brand as much as the product or service. Also, as more users rely on the Web as a strategic business vehicle to the exclusion of other marketing vehicles, the Web experience becomes the brand. (We will explore the implications of the Web on branding in chapter 4.)

Lastly, the dynamic nature of the Web creates an opportunity to transform the communication between the company and the visitor from a one-way communication into an ongoing dialogue. This allows companies to learn more about their prospects and customers so information can be tailored to their interests. Newly evolved Consumption Cycles require that. By hooking prospects and customers into recognizing the value of being known to the Web site—through practices such as requiring registration for updates or technical support (without exploiting them!)—a mutually beneficial dialogue can be established that will ultimately enable the vendor to provide the right solution for customer needs.

SALES

For many types of businesses, the key reason to have a Web presence is to conduct commerce. The Web is well suited to many types of commerce situations, both for businesses and consumers. In this phase of the Consumption Cycle, customers' demands are very straightforward. They want all the information required to make a purchase decision; they want to be able to have access to the full range of products and services they need, to be able to perform transactions in ways with which they are familiar, and to be sure that the transactions are secure.

The Whole Experience philosophy can be summed up by 21st Century Media Partners' Weintraut when he states with aplomb, "We're not in the retail business. We're in the convenience business."

Many companies are reluctant to fully empower customers to perform sales transactions on the Web for several reasons. The process is technically complex, and most existing IT infrastructures weren't designed with the required functionality built in. Therefore, e-commerce capabilities have to be added to existing systems, or systems have to be replaced. But more importantly, companies are stuck in a bind with their distribution strategy. Offering Web e-commerce directly to customers can be disruptive to the sales channel. But in many cases, the disruption in the sales channel can have a positive impact on the customer.

For some industries, the Web is enabling a radical change in the way products are sold. The traditional way we buy cars is a perfect example of an outdated process—it's an inefficient system that consumers despise. Prior to the Internet, consumers had no way of knowing the actual dealer invoice price, manufacturer rebates, or other purchasing incentives. Car dealers liked it that way. Ill-informed prospects are easily manipulated; educated buyers are not.

We started seeing the incentive to change the sales process in this industry when Saturn introduced their "haggle-free" car-buying policy. This popular change in car-buying policy has spilled onto the Web. There are numerous Web sites that have embraced this "friction-free" philosophy and have elevated it to the next level by empowering consumers with a wealth of purchase information. This makes the shopping and purchasing process much more efficient.

Many retailers and manufacturers have also started selling products online. Some start with what we call a "toe-in-the-water" strategy, selling some limited set of products online to test the market's reaction. Unfortunately, this approach can often elicit a negative response, because customers tend to want what they are accustomed to in the analog world to be available online—all at once. If they are disappointed with product selection, they probably won't buy anything. Worst of all, they may not come back to try again. Lesson learned: Tentative approaches can backfire, especially when competitors already offer full-blown access to products and services via the Web.

In the end, customers don't care about the internal struggles of vendors. They care about conducting their business. If other companies in the market are providing the ability to transact sales via the Web, that could be the deciding factor in where the business goes. End of story.

No doubt, the Internet is altering the way products and services are being sold across all industries. And many companies are charging ahead with innovative new sales strategies to capitalize on the vulnerability of the marketplace.

Distribution

Product delivery is another integrated component of the Whole Experience. Today's customers demand a higher level of service throughout the distribution chain: online quoting and configuration, real-time electronic delivery, instant order verification, up-to-date product tracking, and one-click product registration. Performing these functions well is a critical aspect of building trust with your customers.

"ONSALE is investing heavily in enhancing the consumer experience because customers have become more demanding," asserts Alan Fisher, cofounder and chief technology officer at online auctioneer ONSALE. "For example, we send an e-mail within an hour after receiving an order confirming a bid. We also send e-mails updating customers on delivery status."[6]

More and more of today's leading e-commerce companies offer online tracking of products. But those tracking services are only as good as the shipping services offered by companies such as Federal Express, United Parcel Service (UPS), and the U.S. Postal Service (USPS). In fact, for companies in the business of shipping, online tracking has become a must-have to maintain market share.

Both FedEx and UPS, on the other hand, are heavily investing information systems that will give them a competitive advantage. FedEx has been the early leader in this area, first introducing InterNetship in 1996, an innovative, online product tracking service. More recently they rolled out a new software program that allows international businesses in fifty-eight countries to engage in product distribution transactions via the FedEx Web site.[7] Any *www.fedex.com* customer can now access the Federal Express Web site (at whatever time of day is convenient) and request a parcel pickup, find local FedEx drop-off locations, request invoice and delivery location adjustments, print custom shipping labels, and track the status of his deliveries.

UPS offers customers an array of e-commerce related services, including customer shipping and tracking software, complete electronic commerce solutions for small businesses, and productivity tools that can be added to an existing Web site. For

example, UPS Document Exchange helps UPS customers transform paper-based business practices into electronic processes
linked via the Internet. UPS Internet Tools are HTML page code
that allow customers to offer package tracking capability from
their Web sites. UPS OnLine® Solutions is software that allows
customers to easily track client orders and integrate shipping
management procedures through custom UPS application program interfaces (APIs).

USPS offers only basic tracking of overnight mail—a number
is assigned to a package that can be traced by the customer if the
package doesn't show up where it is supposed to. This type of
package tracking is not in real time, meaning that USPS doesn't
really know where a package is at any given time. To find a missing package, they have to recreate the delivery process via a
"paper trail" to uncover where the package is. USPS claims it will
expand this basic tracking system to other types of mail some-
time in 1999.

Our research indicates that the Internet is having a ripple
effect throughout the entire shipping industry. In a recent
Cognitiative Pulse of the Customer focus group, the CIO of a
small shipping/freight company commented that FedEx's aggressive Web strategy had forced his company to follow suit.

Offering online services such as product tracking can be a
benefit to the company as well as to the customer. Dell Computer
reports that prior to its Web site launch, customers called an
average of once or twice per purchase to check on the status of
product delivery. Now, with its online order tracking, customers
check in electronically an average of eight to ten times per order
instead of calling. The online tracking feature of the Dell site is
obviously filling an information void and reducing Dell's costs
from answering phone inquiries.

Web upstarts such as Chemdex have developed highly complex, automatic tracking and notification systems that act as information conduits for every point in the online purchase process.
The Chemdex system ties in to both the FedEx and UPS package
tracking systems, so Chemdex can see when an order is shipped,
track the package for the customer, and alert her if any shipping

delays occur. This empowers customers with a way to respond to such delays (for example, ship the partial order or wait until the entire order is ready). The Chemdex distribution model puts the customer in control of as much of the distribution cycle as possible.

As Chemdex's CEO and founder David Perry asserts, "Companies selling online need to be proactive when it comes to package tracking—rather than waiting for the customer to scream, 'Where is my package?'"

Support

While marketing, sales, and product delivery increasingly become integrated with each other on the Web, customer support often remains the function of a single departmental Web site within a bigger organization. This presents a special challenge for a company looking to build a Whole Experience Web environment. Being easy to do business with—providing access to support, service, news, and information, and creating a sense of community among your customers—are critical actions that need to be taken to build customer loyalty in the online arena. And Internet technologies are enabling companies to offer electronic support via the Web.

Many companies are enjoying significant returns on their online customer service initiatives. For example, 70 percent of Cisco's requests for technical assistance are now handled electronically—allowing the firm to cut costs and retarget that money elsewhere. Web real-estate destination *www.iown.com* is on its way to reducing the costs of serving its customers by 50 percent. And Autodesk, the world's largest design solutions software company, launched an aggressive technical assistance effort via the Web that claims to have seen a 1,600 percent return on investment for the company.

Dell Computer is also using the Web to provide comprehensive and productive customer service. "We've had a great experience with support online, not only from a call reduction standpoint, but from a richness of information that we can deliver," claims Dell Online's Director, Robert Langer.[8] "Many of our customers are turning to the Web site first to try to self-diagnose problems, even on the consumer level. For our corporate customers, through Premier Pages, we link them directly into our help tech databases, which are far more comprehensive in their information than a consumer would see. They utilize that as a first point of contact to get information before they get on the phone with us."

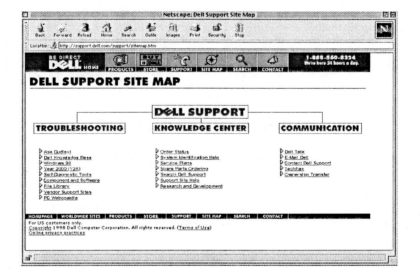

As you can very well guess, the cost savings to Dell is substantial. In early 1999, the number of phone calls that they've eliminated in the order area alone exceeds 50,000 calls a week.

What's so unique and different about online customer support is that it can be a much faster and more efficient way of disseminating crucial "need-to-know" information. When a customer needs help, he needs it immediately, not when it's convenient for the vendor.

Unfortunately, too many companies offer second-rate customer service via the Web. Online features that may benefit these companies do not always benefit their customers. For too many online customers, self-service can often mean no service.

A leading technology magazine once told the story of a major consumer products company that received about 20,000 e-mail messages per month to its customer service center. Only 10 percent of the customer queries received attentive replies (within forty-eight hours); the other 90 percent received nothing for several weeks, because the company regarded customer e-mail as second-class communication.

A Web site should design its online customer service center to provide answers to frequently asked questions (FAQs) twenty-four hours a day, plus answer customer queries on the fly—in real time, when possible. Whole Experience online customer support centers empower and encourage customers to find their own solutions to problems. Our research has shown that the majority of customers not only want to find their own solutions, they often prefer electronic communication to person-to-person interactions. Online support doesn't eliminate the need for human interaction; however, having a knowledgeable person available online is an important element of delivering effective Web-based customer support. In the aggregate, Web-based customer support is a win-win solution for both the company and the customer, one that encourages aftermarket sales and helps increase customer loyalty.

From Generic Experiences to Customized Experiences

Innovative companies have built Whole Experience Web sites that not only pull visitors through the Consumption Cycle but help facilitate the exchange of information, enable electronic commerce, and provide an environment for social interaction. Many of these sites go even further, allowing for personalization and customization—moving from generic experiences to customized experiences that meet the needs of the individual.

One approach is to organize a site by target customer. Companies like Cisco, IBM, Gateway, and Microsoft present users with self-referencing group options such as "Small Businesses," "Developers," and "Enterprises"—all with the notion that the products and information that visitors need will be unique to their type of company or job. This is an important step to creating a Whole Experience Web site, and it makes it easier for the visitor to find what he wants. Internet technology provides many outstanding tools to customize visitors' experiences, such as profiling and dynamic content generation, so that visitors' interests are tracked and content is presented based on their interests.

A Whole Experience Web site goes so far as to anticipate user needs based on data that is collected about them as they interact with the site. Over time, these unique preferences allow a Web site to greet each user by name, serve up personalized marketing messages, stimulate aftermarket sales, and deliver a more satisfying personal experience.

With targeted messaging, many companies have discovered that their online visitors are more likely to buy into techniques such as personalization if the experience actually helps improve business processes. Examples include customized Web sites such as Dell Premier Pages, which contain a customer's required configuration, negotiated pricing, and purchasing policies—simplifying the often tedious and complex process of corporate purchasing. It is important to keep in mind, however, that personalization services are only as good as the general predictions and assumptions they make about the user. And in the work environment, the notion of personalization is a misnomer, since site functionality should be aimed at meeting the customized needs of a user's job functions rather than treating the user as an individual.

Know Thy Market

Many companies who are on the Web assume they know what their customers want and treat Web sites like an afterthought instead of a critical customer relationship business vehicle. But that's exactly the wrong tack to take. Companies should approach Web site development as if they were developing a new product or service, taking all the steps to understand market requirements and customer demands.

"We use the same development process to build our site as we use to build a product," asserts Pamela Roberts, Senior Director, e-business, for Symantec Corporation. "A key component of the process is requirement gathering and research. We hired research companies in the Americas and in Europe to gauge customer opinions on usability, pricing, layout, service, all of that. We developed a list of customer requirements—items they felt were imperative to add to our site. What our customers wanted most was an online experience that provided a two-prong, reseller/direct sales approach. And that's what we're delivering."[9]

The strategy for developing an effective Web presence is similar in many ways to the research conducted during product development. Research can be broken down into six important steps:

1. Survey the market landscape
2. Comprehend target user/customer requirements
3. Determine the needs of prospects
4. Find out what your business partners/allies are doing and how they want to participate
5. Test the usability of the site experience
6. Track satisfaction

SURVEY THE MARKET LANDSCAPE

What's out there already? How high has the bar been set by other businesses in this space? In the context of developing a Web site, companies should learn what their competitors are doing in terms of functionality, look, and feel; the type of user experience they're trying to offer; the interactive features they have; the messages they are promoting—everything.

The great thing about the Web is that you can see what other companies are offering to your markets. But be advised that you can't see what they have in development. Because creating new Web functionality usually has long development lead times, companies should learn about market trends and potential competitive moves from other sources rather than waiting to see it live on the site. Responding to competitive moves after they've been publicly launched can put contenders dangerously behind the curve. Conferences, seminars, trade magazines, and industry analyst reports are valuable for forming a perspective on the market landscape, helping business leaders to understand what competitors are offering or planning to offer, and spotting market trends.

As Dell Online's Langer puts it, "The challenge we face is how to keep pushing the Web initiative ahead every year. From a development standpoint, we tend not to develop anything that has a very long life to it. We want to take on projects that we can turn around quickly—from initial scoping to delivery—within one to two quarters, typically. Get the Web offering up and running and start getting some payback on it right away, as opposed to getting into a multiyear initiative."

COMPREHEND TARGET USER/CUSTOMER REQUIREMENTS

Only direct contact with your customers and prospects will tell you the answers critical to understanding your unique opportunities and meeting customer expectations. What kinds of things do target customers/users want to do on a Web site—not necessarily what do they want to do on any one particular Web site, but in general, how is the Web serving their overall needs for what they want to do? A larger perspective is important because user comments stimulate new creative ideas.

When Cisco Systems decided to seriously invest in a Web presence, a key motivator was to minimize the cost of doing business with its customers, both in terms of sales and customer service costs. In addition, Cisco's management wanted to understand what customers wanted from their service and sales experiences on the Web. To be certain that it was addressing customers' needs, Cisco conducted customer research for its Web site and discovered that its customers wanted to order a broader base of products online. Once their relationship with Cisco was established, they didn't need a salesman calling on them to take orders for certain repeat items. Customers needed a fast and efficient system for purchasing goods and services in their required timeframe. Also, customers wanted to be able to get answers to their questions online instead of calling customer support telephone lines. Cisco found that offering a fully functional Web experience to its customers was a win-win situation. It helped Cisco be more efficient with its business processes, and its customers preferred conducting business via the Web.

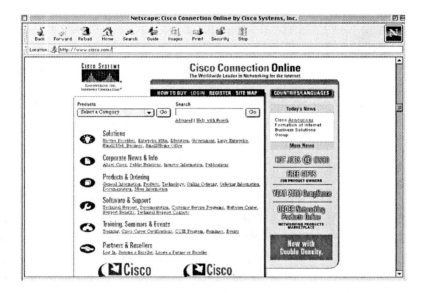

Chemdex, a Web-based life science products aggregator, wanted to change the distribution dynamics of its industry by serving customers in a new way. In response to the needs of the life science industry, it developed a more effective way to manage the procurement of life science research supplies. It found that customers (higher education researchers, biotech laboratories, manufacturers) wanted a single catalog and ordering system with the ability to track orders online and even submit purchase orders. So that's what Chemdex delivered.

A classic comment made about the pitfalls of customer research in the product development cycle is that customers are often limited by their own knowledge of what is possible. There is truth to that observation. Many innovative ideas would never have inspired new products if they had relied on the limited

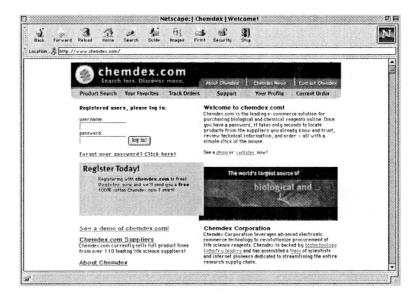

vision of the target customer. So, beyond considering just customers' insights into their Web needs, it is also important to take a further step and analyze what problems of the analog world might be solved with the Web.

For example, Dell discovered that an obstacle for companies, large and small, ordering more products online was the actual purchasing process. Dell realized that a company's purchasing policies needed to be implemented in the online order process to ensure the people placing the orders and the products being ordered were approved. In addition, since companies often don't buy computers with credit cards, Dell needed to enable a purchase order and invoicing process as part of the online experience.

Dell's answer? The Paperless Purchase Order. Business customers sign up on the front end—literally a one-page agreement between the customer and Dell—where they identify a purchase level based on a commitment over the course of a period of time, typically one year. It's similar to a debit card, where there's a balance established against which the customer purchases. Each time customers make a new purchase, there is no requirement to generate a new purchase order. All they do is log onto their Premier Page, enter their Paperless Purchase Order number, and place their order straight into Dell's system. Dell subtracts the purchase amount against the balance of the Paperless Purchase Order. As customers' accounts approach their expiration point or monetary limit, a reminder is sent to them asking if they'd like to re-up the agreement.

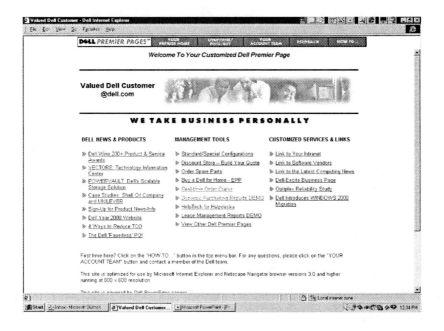

This process is a benefit for customers, because they're streamlining and minimizing the paperwork process and getting their orders entered in more quickly. It's a benefit for Dell, because allowing the customer to tap straight into the company's manufacturing system, removes one-half day to a day and a half from the purchase order entry process. Effectively, the machines are getting manufactured and shipped out more quickly. Paperless Purchase Orders are enabling Dell to move to a guaranteed delivery time environment.

DETERMINE THE NEEDS OF PROSPECTS

What could you offer someone who visits your site that would cause them to become a prospect (someone who is not currently doing businesses with you but who might one day)? How can you improve the "look-to-book" ratio (a metric used in e-commerce to track the purchase decision process)? How can your site explain/position your products and services better than your competitors? How can your Web site get prospects closer to making a purchase decision?

These were issues that Oracle Corporation faced as they set their sights on midsize companies, selling mission-critical, run-the-business financial and manufacturing applications and services. Oracle had traditionally used a direct sales force to sell primarily to large companies. But when they began targeting smaller companies they realized that using the direct sales approach was impractical. There were too many companies to reach and not enough Oracle feet on the street. Oracle thus began building relationships with indirect sales channels. While they felt that indirect channels might be the best way to sell to smaller companies, they knew that indirect channels would benefit from pre-qualification of the prospect.

Oracle decided that its FastForward Web page, a part of its main home page, had to provide prospects with some way of determining that certain Oracle solutions would fit their needs before they engaged a salesperson. And the site needed to proactively notify Oracle and its channel partners of interested prospects who wanted to be contacted. This self-qualifying mechanism had to go beyond "brochureware"—it had to be able to empower prospects with the ability to determine for themselves which solutions were right for them. The resulting interactive, self-qualifying Web site helps prospective customers to determine if Oracle is a candidate to meet their needs. And it also serves as a mechanism to notify a sales channel when an interested company is ready to be contacted.

Another example is Amazon.com, which works very hard to transform prospects into customers by offering discounted sales, first-time buyer shipment upgrades, and money-back guarantees on any item ordered online. Amazon knows that it is very expensive to get someone to come to its site, due to the advertising required to attract enough traffic. Because of this, it focuses intently, not only on capturing, but on maintaining the business of its visitors as well.

FIND OUT WHAT YOUR BUSINESS PARTNERS/ALLIES ARE DOING AND HOW THEY WANT TO PARTICIPATE

One of the trickiest aspects of doing business on the Web is managing existing partnerships. (This topic is discussed from a business strategy context in chapter 3.) Many companies are struggling with how to maintain positive relationships with their partners in an online world. The issues are very legitimate. One scenario is to work with business partners to create integrated solutions that benefit both parties.

Many companies have worked out approaches that integrate their partners into their Web solution. For example, Cisco has a system where participating resellers are compensated for orders booked online with Cisco, as long as the resellers perform functions such as product delivery, logistics, and onsite installation. Oracle's site promotes the solutions of its Business Alliance Partners and provides links to their sites for more information.

Quantum Corporation, a manufacturer of computer storage products and technologies, has created a Web site outside of its company's firewall, so that its partners can receive equal representation as providers of storage solutions based on Quantum's digital linear tape technology (DLTtape). Quantum's Web site is a symbol of partnership in its community and ultimately provides customers a host of competitive alternatives from which to choose.

TEST THE USABILITY OF THE SITE EXPERIENCE

Before a company rolls out a new corporate Web site or rechristens an existing site with new functionality, it should test user response to the material in advance of the launch in order to make any adjustments to the site that may be needed. Research has shown that people respond very differently to a new idea when they actually experience it versus when they are merely told about it. It's always amazing to see what emerges in usability testing (conducting site prototype tests with target users in a controlled setting) compared to the assumptions that are made in the Web site design phase.

Dell's Langer agrees, "Every quarter, we survey our customers online. And we conduct usability tests on a regular basis, whether we're testing new features and functions or looking at new ways of improving product delivery."

Don't assume that just because a Web site is intended to be easy to use, it actually is. Usability testing is often necessary to provide a company with critical data about all elements of the experience, such as reactions to specific content, navigation, and design elements. User feedback actually becomes a prerequisite to successful site development going forward. Some usability test labs are set up to record how long users stay in certain areas of the site, the sequence of activities performed, what they click on first, and what they ignore. These insights are extremely valuable in creating an experience that users find productive and fulfilling.

TRACK SATISFACTION

After a Web site has been developed, a company must commit to a site-monitoring strategy to ensure that the online experience continually meets the needs of its users. There are a couple of basic methods used to monitor user satisfaction of a Web site: "contact us" feedback mechanisms, where customers proactively click on a "feedback" icon and send a message to the site administrators; and direct customer contact via surveys or focus groups.

User feedback is useful, but unsolicited comments submitted by a small percentage of visitors do not always represent a cross section of typical site visitors. Feedback is often limited to extreme viewpoints—both critical and constructive—and tends to represent extremes of the population, such as your loyal customer zealots and the dreaded ax grinders. It's important for a company to listen to its users, but these feedback mechanisms should not be the only way a company monitors the effectiveness of its online efforts.

Online surveys are mechanisms whereby site visitors answer a series of questions in some detail about what they liked and didn't like about a site. Surveys can provide site administrators with much richer depth of content than responses gathered from standard feedback forms. And surveys allow companies to choose the topics on which they want to focus the research.

As with unsolicited feedback, the problem with online surveys is also self-selection sample bias—the respondents who are willing to fill out questionnaires do not spread across the entire customer population, although they are not usually as extreme as the unsolicited feedback providers. Web surveys must take sample selection bias into account, because the results may give a skewed picture of the actual results. Direct contact through phone surveys and focus groups can provide rich additional information, and it is advisable to use these methods at some affordable frequency. Whatever the mechanism, the task of site monitoring is never truly completed, because customers' expectations change as they become more Web-savvy.

Some Caveats about Research

Some companies study their markets and their customers too much. Instead of helping to solve problems, research often seems to invoke decision paralysis. Such companies hide behind research as a way to avoid making difficult, risky decisions. In these situations, research is a business inhibitor rather than an enabler.

However, some companies don't study at all. They often believe that they know their markets best and that there's nothing to be gained from research. Sometimes they are right, other times they're not. It's a big gamble.

The best approach, of course, is to create balance. If you are looking to integrate the Web into your business, spend some resources on researching your customers. Never assume you know what your customers will say—you'd be surprised at what they will reveal to third parties about your company, your products, and your services. It pays to find out. Base your Web development strategies partly on what you learn through research and partly on what you believe, especially in testing new concepts or ideas. Customers, influencers, and prospects will always be limited by their own experience and imagination. Sometimes a company must lead the way with bold new programs—and the Web is a great testing ground for these ideas.

The most productive and engaging Web sites are those that have made the effort to get to know their visitors, using research to identify common user attitudes or commissioning formative usability tests to discover what areas of the site are most effective. Armed with this critical data, companies can better understand why people come to their site, what actions they take when they are there, and where they are in the Consumption Cycle. This knowledge can then be used to develop a proactive strategy that satisfies user needs.

Epilogue: The Human Touch is Still Required

Despite the fervor for Web sites as strategic vehicles, it is important to keep in mind that some human contact is still required, even for successful Web businesses. Many companies believe that human relationships, personal accountability, and artful negotiations are essential to the long-term success of any Web effort.

For example, both Cisco and Dell, two companies with extremely successful Web operations, continue to negotiate the majority of their business relationships with customers via direct sales representatives and then use the Web to implement the terms, conditions, and policies of the relationship. The human element is not eliminated, but it focuses the human interaction on key, value-add aspects and allows the Web to perform the routine functions of the arrangement.

"People will always be involved in hammering out a contract agreement face-to-face," claims Dell's Langer. "Even the most ardent online enthusiasts are not going to make those kinds of purchasing decisions passively over a Web site. But once you've locked those agreements in place, you can leverage that deal and take advantage of it through a Web site."

Similarly, Preview Travel enables its customers to shop for, "preview," and purchase vacations. Even though the majority of Preview's customer requests are handled via email, there is always a customer service representative standing by to resolve questions or concerns, if needed. The number of telephone calls the company receives is not growing as rapidly as transactions are growing—and the majority of customers seem satisfied being serviced electronically.

In recent research with corporate procurement managers, we found that these professionals were concerned about removing the "human element" from their daily business duties. Many believe that human interface will always be important to their work. For some of these people, the Web, while playing a key role in procurement, will never totally replace the human aspects of corporate purchasing.

On the other hand, some people want to replace the human element. IT managers see avoiding human contact as a plus, as they are inundated with continual telesales calls. The Web solves this problem by empowering IT managers to configure and order their own product lines and find their own answers to problems they may have.

"In some cases, the Web enables businesses to provide better customer service, while in other cases, businesses do a much worse job online than they did previously," says RealSelect's CEO Stuart Wolff. "It really depends on the customer and the type of service being offered. There are some customers that don't like interacting with humans, so the Internet is a better way for them to get the information they need. There are other customers who don't like interacting with systems and only want to interact with humans, so the Web is not a good communications medium for them."[10]

Wolff tells a story about Fred Rosen, founder of Ticketmaster, who, when first told of the potential for doing business online, was dead against using the Web as a consumer business medium. Some of his subordinates finally talked him into launching an electronic commerce site online, and Ticketmaster sold its first online concert ticket shortly thereafter. The company phoned the inaugural customer—a man in Washington State—and asked him why he used the Internet to buy a ticket. The man replied, "Because I don't like talking to people, and I don't like talking to you." And he hung up. That story says it all.

Today's businesses face the difficult challenge of migrating complex consumption behaviors to the Web without alienating or confusing their existing customer base. It's clear that many customers are willing to move in this direction, but they need the guidance of visionary companies to help lead the way.

Chapter Three

Resolve Conflict with Existing Business Strategies

"Existing businesses must not only move to the Web, they must do it quickly before their competitors if they hope to take advantage of this discontinuous innovation."

—David Perry, Founder and CEO, Chemdex Corporation

The greatest challenge in responding to the Web dilemma is in comprehending, reconciling, and executing the changes in existing business models brought about by the Web. Clearly, providing Whole Experience Web sites to suspects, prospects, and customers—as discussed in chapter 2—touches every corner of an organization and its mode of business. For some areas within companies, the change will be easy to absorb. For others the Web represents a strategic upheaval.

Of course, each company has its own unique business model—how revenue is generated, the way sales initiatives are promoted, the way employees are compensated, the way partners are selected, and so on. But there are a few things all companies have in common. First, all companies must be vigilant in making sure that their offerings are available where the customers want to buy them. That's been a fundamental business principle since the beginning of commerce. Second, no organization can afford to ignore the Web. Every company should be either contemplating or executing a Web-based sales strategy.

So what should businesses that are dependent on conventional delivery systems do when customers demand to be served through the Web? What happens to a business organization that is totally geared towards a traditional channel pipeline, pushing product through distributors so they can in turn sell to retailers?

In this chapter, we'll look at some examples of how companies have dealt with these issues, ranging from radical business strategy changes to evolving complementary changes. We discuss distribution models that have developed, and we look at emerging Web distribution channels.

Real World Examples

While still a relatively new phenomenon, the Web has already created substantial strategic change for many companies. Some companies, such as Egghead Software and Encyclopaedia Brittannica, made a radical change. American Express experimented with American Express Interactive. Barnes and Noble created a spin-off company. Fidelity, Dell, and Marshall Industries extended their value propositions into cyberspace while maintaining their traditional modes of doing business. Let's take a closer look at how these companies did this.

For over ten years, Egghead Software operated a chain of 170 boutique software stores throughout the United States.[1] They battled it out with stores such as Software Etc. and Babbages, each vying for a small piece of the retail pie. But by the early 1990s, there was a boom in competition as computer superstores, discount warehouses, and mass catalogers sprouted up across the country, siphoning business—and profits—from the Eggheads of the world. And it appeared as if the Web and the proliferation of online shopping ventures would intensify competition.

In 1997 Egghead faced a difficult crossroads in its business road map. Egghead was having a hard time turning a profit through small retail stores located in shopping malls. In fact, business got so bad that the company closed about half its stores and focused its efforts on developing an electronic commerce Web site, in hopes that the Internet might be a better way to create sales growth and increase sagging profits. The results of Egghead's early online efforts were encouraging, so much so that the company acquired Surplus Direct and Surplus Auction. Management then decided that the best course of action for Egghead was to abandon the traditional retail market altogether and move its entire business operation onto the Web. The company had an established brand name plus significant cash reserves to implement the new business strategy. It also had the vision of skilled executive managers ready to lead the charge. It closed all of its retail outlets, designed an Internet sales strategy, and changed its name to Egghead.com.

The company forged marketing alliances with popular Internet players, such as America Online, ZDNet, eBay, Netscape, CNET's Shopper.com, and Microsoft in an attempt to rapidly build its electronic commerce brand and site traffic. Egghead.com focused all of its energies on making sure that its value proposition and brand promise were translated to the online world. The company utilized its customer list of one million e-mail addresses to jumpstart its marketing efforts. It brought together its three separate online destinations (*www.egghead.com, www.surplusdirect.com,* and *www.surplusauction.com*) into one online super site. It launched an aggressive offline advertising campaign, including television, magazine, and newspaper advertising. Its theme, "Shop three times smarter," coincided with its overall business strategy and online advertising program.

So far, the results are encouraging—Egghead.com's growth has been substantial. Its second quarter results for fiscal year 1999 showed a 73 percent increase in revenue from the comparable period the year before. It also saw its number of auction bidders nearly double and its e-mail database rise 14 percent. However, the firm does not expect to be profitable for several years to come.

Encyclopaedia Britannica (EB) is an example of a traditional company that had to reconfigure its entire sales process in the face of rising public demand for access to information via the Internet. In fact, EB is making more money online than it ever did in the offline world. In the old days, the firm sold hardcover volumes of its encyclopedia door-to-door. Years later, salespeople worked from sales leads that were generated from various forms of direct-response advertising, such as TV and direct mail, and then visited the homes of people who had expressed some form of interest in the product line.

EB began publishing its products on the Internet because it saw an opportunity to add value to the information published in its print encyclopedias—adding such features as full text searching, hypertext linking, and links to other sources of information.[2] EB was the first encyclopedia on the Internet in 1994, at a time when few other publishers were thinking beyond CD-ROM.

EB currently offers two Web services: Britannica Online (*www.eb.com*), an electronic encyclopedia service, and eBLAST, a Web navigation and search service (*www.eBLAST.com*). Britannica Online sells annual "site licenses" to institutions, such as schools, libraries, and universities, and charges by the number of students or patrons that have access to the service. The institution makes the service available to all these users on their desktops. Individuals can also get personal subscriptions to Britannica Online; eBLAST is supported by advertising and sponsorships.

American Express, a global company that operates the world's largest travel agency, has built a thriving business out of assisting companies in managing and controlling their business travel and general expenses. The company is experimenting with the Web in an attempt to extend this value proposition into cyberspace. In November 1997, American Express Interactive (AXI), a division of American Express, in conjunction with Microsoft Corporation, launched a customized business travel destination site branded as AXI Travel. The service extends the company's business model onto the Web while simultaneously protecting the company's installed base from possible Web competitors.

AXI Travel enables corporate travelers to book their own travel reservations within the parameters of a company's own corporate policy. For example, the AXI Travel site can be branded with a corporate logo, configured to meet a company's corporate travel policies, and integrated with preferred vendors. AXI operates over the Internet or via an extranet using a dedicated frame-relay connection (a secure method of transferring information from one system to another). Corporate travelers access AXI from their PCs, using a standard Web browser.

AXI's online reservations are fully integrated with the service provided by dedicated American Express travel agency locations, so companies are ensured that their travel policies are applied consistently, regardless of whether their employees make reservations online or via telephone with a travel agent. In early 1999 approximately four hundred corporate clients with over 400,000 unique users signed up to the AXI service.

Yvonne Schneider, director of American Express Corporate Services Interactive, says of the American Express Web strategy, "To be successful on the Web, companies need to make their Web service offerings easy to use, easy to adopt, with plenty of incentives to lure customers onboard."[3]

Fidelity Investments is a good example of a company that adopted the Web to extend its service options. The firm launched its trading Web site in January 1997 to augment its traditional investment and financial services and to defend its turf from upstarts such as E*Trade. Being a full service investment services firm, part of the company's philosophy is the belief that different types of customers prefer different methods of trading. Therefore, Fidelity's strategy is to retain existing customers who prefer doing business online as well as attract new, incremental business to the firm through its online presence. Because customers have a wide range of service preferences, Fidelity management believes that the company's online offering does not cannibalize other methods of stock trading. In the long-term, Fidelity's management is confident that some financial services, such as estate planning, will always require human interaction, so the company continues to offer these types of services in person—even to the online investor.

Barnes and Noble, a classic offline retail player, is a good example of a company that was forced to migrate to the Internet and, in doing so, changed its business and ownership structure. The bookstore chain initially perceived electronic commerce as a threat. Barnes and Noble was, and is, heavily invested in bricks-and-mortar establishments. Driving traffic into their company-owned retail stores was key to their return on investment (ROI). But the rapid acceptance and enthusiasm for online book retailing, driven by Amazon.com, became alarming. The company was faced with a tough choice—both strategically and financially. The company needed to compete in both worlds—physically and virtually. Yet, the investments required to be competitive in both worlds overwhelmed its traditional business model. Ultimately, founder and CEO Leonard Riggio decided that to compete effectively on the Web, Barnes and Noble must be able to play on a more level playing field with Amazon.com. Therefore, it formed a spin-off company, barnesandnoble.com, sold 50 percent ownership to German publishing firm Bertelsmann AG, and did an internal purchase order (IPO) in 1999.

Marshall Industries (*www.marshall.com*) is an example of a company that predicted that its technical market customers would prefer online business and leveraged the Internet as a strategic business vehicle very early in the emergence of the Web. The company is one of the largest global distributors of industrial electronic components and production supplies in the world, selling semiconductors, connectors, test equipment, computer systems and peripherals, tool kits, and workstations. In 1994, the visionary president and CEO of Marshall Industries, Robert Rodin, realized the Web's ability to proliferate all segments of the business-to-business market. Today, Marshall Industries runs one of the most efficient (and award-winning) business commerce sites on the Internet.

Marshall's Web site provides customers with a full range of Internet services, from shopping for hundreds of technical products, to real-time ordering of products, to interactive training sessions and product seminars, to online technical support. Customers can search the site by product description, part number, or manufacturer. They can order, purchase, and track the status of their orders. The site even offers users a service called QuoteCart, where customers can submit a long list of parts or an entire bill of materials via the Web site and get a quote with the click of a mouse. Marshall is also one of the only companies in the world to regularly broadcast live voice data and video seminars to customers and business partners in twenty-seven languages over the Internet through its subsidiary, ENEN.com.

It's obvious that Marshall Industries is doing something right. "I think our efforts have been successful—we've seen an increase in business due to our Web presence, but we are really on a journey," says Marshall's Rodin. "We listen to our customers and always try to anticipate their needs. The beauty of Web interaction and twenty-four-hour-a-day coverage is that we are getting feedback up to the minute. We can alter our service and capabilities as people use our site. This has given us enormous competitive leverage. Our Web site has been a beta test site for many new capabilities. People recognize us for our online efforts, and we attract a lot of attention for our new ideas. It definitely gives us an advantage to be at the forefront of change."[4]

When Dell Computer shook up the PC industry by utilizing the 1-800 number as its direct sales channel and selling record quantities of computers, its competitors took notice. Dell has now extended its direct model to the Internet as a means of selling its products to its customers, and its foray into the world of electronic commerce has been quite successful. Dell's sales strategy has forced its competitors, such as Compaq, IBM, and Hewlett Packard, to venture into the e-commerce world themselves.

In late 1998, Dell Online's Director, Robert Langer, said, "We are doing in excess of $6 million a day through our Web site, and that's during a sevenday week. That comes out to about $14 million per day. In terms of where that shakes out percentagewise, it's approximately 18 to 19 percent of our total business that's occurring online. We still have a ways to go to hit our goal, which we've set for the end of 2000, to at least half of our total business online. Right now, it's probably split pretty evenly between consumer and business-to-business. Our future growth on the Web will take us more in the direction of serving the business-to-business market, which would more accurately mirror Dell's overall profile, which is about 85 percent business trade."

These companies are among many who have realized that embracing the Web is not only a competitive strategy, but increasingly a market requirement. The stories of how they approached their adoption of the Web illustrates that there are many creative and evolving ways of being a Web-involved company. Regardless of approach, they share a common realization—the risk to not change was as great as the risk to change.

"The Web is changing the way businesses compete," asserts Chemdex's Perry. "Companies like Mary Kay Cosmetics and Amway should have an advantage in the market because they have relationships with customers and suppliers through their huge sales force. They have lots of resources at their disposal. Their biggest problem is that they've succeeded using only one businesses model—and business models are hard to change. How does Mary Kay get rid of all its sales associates or transform its business operation without destroying what it already has?"

Many other businesses that are locked into traditional business processes are also about to undergo a radical transformation invoked by the Web. "Companies who *don't* think the Web will have a significant impact on their business are either naive or crazy," claims Wolff, of RealSelect. "There are a handful of businesses that might not need a Web presence—but they're operating extremely niche businesses."

Key Questions to Ask Yourself

Executing successful Web strategies requires companies to walk a fine line between pursuing aggressive online business practices and simultaneously improving offline relationships with existing partners, suppliers, distributors, and salespeople. Leveraging Whole Experience online environments to streamline sales and procurement processes, simplifying customer support, and encouraging repeat purchases cuts across every part of a company and touches essentially every business relationship.

To develop the Web strategy, today's executive management must face difficult questions, such as:

1. Should we sell our product directly to customers over the Internet?
2. If we do, will our channels retaliate by refusing to continue selling our products?
3. If we sell our products online, should we sell our products at a discount or at list price? How will this decision impact our channel relationships?
4. In an online business, what do we "give away" versus charge for?
5. If we sell our own products directly to customers, how will we handle product fulfillment and customer support?
6. How will revenue streams shift due to a Web strategy? How soon will we generate revenue?
7. How should we compensate our internal salespeople who might lose commission income as the Web cuts them out of the buying process?
8. How do we transition from our current business model to include an online business model—without disruption?

Benefits of Online Customer Relationships to the Vendor

Whole Experience Web sites, when developed effectively, can offer myriad benefits to target site visitors. But what about the benefits to you, the vendor? Obviously, defending your installed base of customers and sustaining your market position has its benefits. But the Web business model offers some new and very powerful benefits to those who do a good job of implementing Whole Experience Web sites. These are important to under-stand—not only to know how your own company can benefit, but also to understand what your online competition has at its dis-posal. Benefits documented by Web site pioneers such as Cisco, Dell, Preview Travel, and Amazon.com include:

- Generates new and better sales leads. Provides a mechanism where suspects can qualify themselves without requiring sales representatives to call on them.
- Increases aftermarket sales volume. The Web encourages aftermarket sales and stimulates repeat business when customers are electronically notified of special promotions, new product upgrades, or new product releases.
- Reduces cost of sales. Automated order processing helps to eliminate order errors. Features such as electronic tracking allow for greater inventory control, resulting in greater efficiencies in cycle time. Fewer salespeople are needed to facilitate the sales process. Less administrative personnel are needed to process orders. There are lower marketing costs to fulfill requests for information. Better sales lead qualification makes sales efforts better hit ratios. Higher volumes lead to lower cost per sale.
- Decreases support costs with online technical support; more customer questions are answered and problems are resolved without human intervention, decreasing the number of telephone calls and telephone support personnel.
- Provides sales intelligence by capturing user/customer feedback and preferences. If the underlying technology of a corporate Web site is configured to do so, the site can automatically capture sales and marketing intelligence about its visitors so that offers can be more targeted, resulting in higher "look-to-book" ratios.
- Provides better service to smaller accounts that cannot be economically served through traditional offline channels. The Web is a universal equalizer that empowers businesses with the ability to offer multiple levels of quality service and support to all customers, regardless of size, at a price that makes good business sense.
- Improves customer retention and customer satisfaction by providing required services, stimulating repeat business, and efficiently addressing specific customer needs.

Typical Online Distribution/Sales Models

The benefits of the Web are many, but how well a Web site delivers these benefits is dependent on the distribution/sales model a company adopts. Not all models are equal in delivering benefits. There are basically four types of sales models employed on the Web today: Promote and Point; Limited Selling and Lots of Pointing; Sell and Point; and Strategic Selling.

Strategy #1: Promote and Point

Promote and Point sites provide lots of useful product information and often look and feel like online catalogs. They drive the customer partway through the purchase decision cycle but then stop. Unfortunately for the customer, these sites do not allow the user to buy the product or service online. Instead, the site points the user to a sales channel that resells the products.

This approach is often seen in the apparel industry. As of early 1999, Birkenstock Footprint Sandals (*www.birkenstock.com*), a company that sells nearly 2 million pairs of German sandals annually in the United States through retailers, licensed shops, and company-owned stores, doesn't yet sell footwear from its Web site. Liz Claiborne (*www.lizclaiborne.com*), a top maker of clothes and accessories for career-oriented women, does not yet sell its wares online, although the firm claims to be studying its sales options. Instead, these companies look to their retailers to extend e-commerce to the end customer, an approach that many in their industry take.

Some companies have improved on this Promote and Point model by adding a valuable service. For example, InsWeb created a service that helps customers shop for insurance conveniently and securely without sales pressure. InsWeb doesn't actually sell the insurance—the insurance carriers sell the insurance through traditional means. InsWeb allows consumers to comparison shop for auto, term life, homeowner's, renter's, health, and a variety of other insurance products, plus receive quotes tailored to their specific needs from some of the top insurance carriers, including State Farm, Progressive, Nationwide, CNA, and Liberty Mutual.

Consumers can click on each company and see their value proposition. After reviewing the online quotes, consumers can request coverage from one of the carriers. InsWeb forwards requests to the selected insurance carrier, which then contacts the consumer direct, either over the phone, through e-mail, or regular mail. It's up to the carrier and consumer to finalize an actual insurance policy agreement.

The Promote and Point approach to selling has its risks. The success of the strategy depends, to a large degree, on the integrity of your channel partners—and whether or not those partners can adequately deliver on your brand promise. As long as they live up to their end of the bargain, this strategy can work well for many types of companies.

STRATEGY #2: LIMITED SELLING AND LOTS OF POINTING

Limited Selling and Lots of Pointing Web sites offer customers lots of online purchasing options but limit the scope or variety of products and services from which to choose. This Web sales strategy is growing in popularity because it satisfies many companies' desire to sell close-out items, parts and replacement components, accessories, and other specialty items not available at retail that the customer expects to be able to purchase from the original manufacturer. Customers looking to purchase items not offered for sale online are pointed to an offline sales channel.

For some companies, this strategy is a short-term experiment for a more comprehensive online sales effort. For others, whose channel partners are resisting online direct sales efforts, the "limited selling, lots of pointing" sales strategy is a compromise solution to channel conflict issues.

Who is embracing this type of sales strategy? Nintendo (*www.nintendo.com*) sells replacement components and accessories from its Web site. However, customers who wish to purchase Nintendo's popular video games are directed to mail order companies, retail stores, and online retailers.

Apparel and shoe manufacturer, Kenneth Cole (*www.kennethcole.com*), is another company that offers a limited selection of its apparel online (mainly its top selling items). Prospects and customers who wish to purchase other Kenneth Cole brand goods must visit a local retail store or order via mail order catalog.

Pioneer Electronics USA, Inc. (*www.pioneer.com*) uses its Web site to sell items previously available only to the Japanese market (portable computers and other electronic devices) and items previously sold direct to manufacturers (such as stereo speakers). The firm does not plan on selling products on its Web site that are currently offered via retail channels in the U.S. market.

Even Apple Computer adopted this type of sales strategy when it first released its iMac computer. Instead of selling the highly anticipated new computer system direct from its online store, Apple chose to use its Web site to drive iMac customers to participating retailers. After several months of selling the iMac exclusively through its retail channels, Apple eventually gave consumers the choice of either buying the iMac direct from Apple or purchasing the computer system through a local retailer.

The plus side of this type of sales strategy is that it allows companies to experiment, helping them to understand what's required to do business via the Web. But the "toe-in-the-water" strategy can easily backfire. If sales volumes are lower than expected from this "limited" online offering, company management may get discouraged or even back away from a Web commitment, based on a faulty, half-hearted attempt to sell online. A company may also risk alienating its customers. Customers who come to your site to buy your products may come away from the experience dissatisfied—and choose not to return to your Web site the next time they're looking to buy your products or services.

Strategy #3: Sell and Point

Many companies are promoting a dual strategy where they sell from their own Web sites and through other channels' partners. The notion is to ensure that the product is where people want to buy it—and so customers can choose their preferred sales channel. For example, Sun Microsystem (*www.sun.com*), a leading maker of UNIX-based workstation computers, storage devices, and servers for powering corporate computer networks, has a business-to-business Web site that contains content that informs customers of a variety of ways to purchase its hardware, software, training, education, and consulting products. Prospects can order online, by phone, from the nearest reseller, or through government programs and special leasing programs.

Outdoor recreation and sporting goods supply company Recreational Equipment Incorporated (better known as REI) is a company that successfully added an online sales option to its channel mix. REI stores are often clustered in major metropolitan areas and do not extend into smaller towns. Rather than cannibalizing the efforts of its retail stores, REI's Web site (*www.rei.com*) has enabled the company to reach out geographically to a whole new audience of potential buyers. REI's site is increasing sales while improving customer relations at the same time. REI customers like the around-the-clock convenience of ordering and tracking products online. They appreciate the fact that the online store has gone the extra mile to ensure that the cyber buying experience is analogous to the retail buying experience, and they believe that online customer service is easier and more convenient than similar, offline processes.

Symantec Corporation (*www.symantec.com*), the leading antivirus and data protection software firm, is another company that is taking a multiprong approach to the channel sales issue—supporting as many options as feasible to better serve the needs of its customers. The company realizes that traditional channels may be driving revenue today, but it is the customer, the end-user, who will dictate the way companies sell products tomorrow. Symantec deals with minimizing channel conflict by not competing with its partners on price.

"The Internet opened up an avenue for us that we never had before," says Roberts, of Symantec. "It never made sense for us to sell direct to the end-user except through direct mail because it was just too expensive. There really was no cost-effective way for us to reach our target buyers other than through the retail and existing sales channels. But now we have a cost-effective way to reach that audience, and the Web is that channel."

Symantec knows that many customers like the idea of buying direct from a manufacturer. Other customers prefer to go to a third party, such as Micro Warehouse or Cyberian Outpost, because they have a variety of computer equipment, software, and supplies for sale. Symantec had to address both types of customer preferences without alienating its channels.

"Our philosophy with the channel has been very open. They know we have a Web site, they know we sell direct, they know we are selling at a price that won't undercut them, and we'll commit to that. And, the feedback that we get from our resellers is fine. People are very understanding of this. They may not all like it, but they do understand that it is a reality that vendors do sell from their Web sites. This is a phenomenon that goes way beyond the software industry," says Roberts.

The approach adopted by Symantec can be an upside for its channels. "Statistics from Cyber Dialog on 'Total Internet Influenced Consumer Shopper Revenue' say that 56 percent of the people who shopped online for a product actually purchased the product from a retail store," continues Roberts. "It is statistically proven that people will shop online and go to stores, too. That's why our philosophy is not to undercut our channel prices."

STRATEGY #4: STRATEGIC SELLING

Many companies are developing Web strategies to augment their direct sales efforts, particularly to large, "strategic" customers— an approach we call strategic selling. Leading companies such as Boeing, Intel, and Cisco Systems are high profile examples. Between 1997 and 1998, Boeing Company is reported to have booked $100 million in spare parts from airlines through its Web site. In late 1998, when Intel launched its first commerce site for corporate customers, more than $1 billion of business had moved to the new system within its first fifteen days. Cisco sells over 70 percent of its products via its online presence.

For companies such as these, the Web has not decimated the traditional sales channel—especially in the high dollar, high involvement product area—but it has created a new synergy and balance between direct sales and e-commerce that is critical to sustaining customer satisfaction and improving profit margins. This part of the market has reacted differently because highly complex, high involvement products often require a certain amount of skill on the salesperson's part—especially on the front-end of a customer relationship. The Web won't cause the demise of the salesperson in this type of sales transaction, but there is an opportunity to leverage the Web to surround the initial sales process so that it becomes more efficient, cost effective, and pro-ductive for both the customer and the seller. And the Web plays a key role in aftermarket sales to existing customers as well.

How has the Web impacted the initial sales process in a high involvement transaction? Take a hypothetical traditional pur-chase decision process for procuring an air-conditioning system for an office building as an example. The customer first needs to find out about the particular products that are available and that meet her unique needs. This may involve attending a trade show to gather literature about the vendors and their products as well as talking to sales reps. Various vendors will send collateral material and have salespeople follow up via telephone. After one or more inperson sales presentations and meetings, the sale is finalized.

When you factor the Web into the picture, the Web plays the role of information facilitator—eliminating the need for the prospect/customer to attend the trade show or sift through sales brochures. A Whole Experience Web site can provide those expe-riences electronically and even target messages to meet the exact requirements of each individual visitor to the site. What the Web does very well is condense the early phases of the Consumption Cycle—it facilitates those front-end marketing processes to short-en the sales cycle. In these situations, the highly compensated sales rep's time is focused on providing value-added services and closing the deal. This is just one aspect of how the Web plays a role in strategic selling.

Many companies are successfully using the Web as an after-market sales tool—to capitalize on sales after the initial purchase is made. Both Cisco and Dell use the Web to manage the customer relationship and the reordering process. How companies implement this strategy varies. But companies who are using the Internet as a tool to introduce efficiency into the sales process are providing their customers with a fast and productive way to order more products. Repeat buyers don't need to be "sold." They already have a relationship with the company, and in many instances, they already know what they want to buy. Dealing with a human salesperson does not speed up or enhance the buying process in any significant way. What these customers seem to prefer is a quick and easy way to purchase these items. The Internet, with its twenty-four hour access, seven days a week, is a powerful medium to facilitate this transaction.

"A company like Cisco Systems has done a fantastic job," says Barry Peters, director of marketing for ONSALE. "They understand the value of customer care, and they've designed an Internet frontend that addresses those customer concerns at the point of entry. They've really thought about their channel, and they know when the Web is useful and when a direct sales force is more appropriate."[5]

What must a company's Web effort deliver to facilitate the aftermarket sale? Based on Cognitiative's research with business-to-business customers, a business-to-business Web site needs to be able to offer the kinds of things that address the way the business' customers handle purchasing. Companies will need to figure out how these procedures can be adapted to a Web-based transaction environment—which may mean learning how customers issue purchase orders, developing solutions that monitor purchasing authority levels, and modifying company/vendor invoicing systems to work in an online environment.

Determining how to fulfill these demands is required to adapt a "strategic" selling model in the way Cisco, Dell, and Intel have done. And that can be very hard to implement—not because it's so difficult conceptually, but because there are legacy systems throughout the supply chain that are performing all those functions in a nonintegrated, computing infrastructure.

Determining which of these four distribution/sales models is right for your company is a function of your market and your market research—what your customers want and what your competitors are offering. The decision on whether or not the Web will replace or simply augment time-honored channels in your industry is not entirely in the company's hands. It's ultimately a decision that will be made by the customer.

Channel Chaos

With all of these new strategies for reaching customers, there's no doubt that the Web is creating chaos in the full spectrum of sales and distribution. How the chaos resolves itself will be a function of clever strategy and business stamina.

There are some industries where the traditional channel no longer provides enough value—at least for some parts of the market. Travel is one of them. The travel business has been deeply impacted by the Internet. Traditionally, travel agents controlled access to travel information via services such as Sabre online reservation terminals—a service that was licensed exclusively to authorized travel agents. But the balance of power has changed. Companies such as Internet-upstart Preview Travel have fully integrated flight timetables, fares, and reservations on the Web, allowing customers to custom assemble and book their own travel itineraries. Preview Travel's integrated online service, and others like it, have displaced the traditional role of travel agents, who previously "owned" access to this type of information.

The growing use of the Web as a strategic commerce tool should not come as a surprise. "Nonstore" retailing (selling without the use of stores, such as through direct mail catalogs) has been a growing trend for many years. In fact, many analysts forecast that between 25 and 30 percent of all general merchandise sold in the United States today can be attributed to nonstore retailing.

"Big manufacturing companies are looking for ways to go around wholesalers and reach their customers direct," claims

Wolff of RealSelect, the parent company of Realtor.com. "They've been looking for that for a long time. The Internet presents an opportunity to go consumer-direct. Even for manufacturers who are working with their wholesale distributors and not looking for ways to circumvent these middlemen, the Web presents an opportunity to restructure the process of buying and selling goods."

What is the likelihood that the Internet will displace bricks-and-mortar intermediaries such as agents and brokers? Realtor.com's Wolff suggests six key factors that will influence that possibility:

- Size of the transaction
- Frequency of the transaction
- Number of current intermediaries
- Complexity and speed of the task
- Information aspect of the transaction
- Homogeneity of the transaction

Wolff suggests that intermediaries who perform simple, smaller, and mundane tasks requiring quick turnaround time stand a greater chance of being displaced by a Web-based solution. Likewise, companies performing very large or complex services/transactions have less risk of being displaced by an Internet intermediary.

Some companies aggressively moved into selling online without informing the channel in advance and met with some disastrous results. Gibson Musical Instruments (*www.gibson.com*), the leading maker of guitars and other musical instruments for the past hundred years, is an example of a company who followed this path and then reversed its course. It launched an initiative to sell its guitars from its Web site at 10 percent below list price. It seemed like a smart idea. The Internet was a relatively inexpensive way to connect directly to the consumer, gather demographic data, build brand loyalty, and potentially, increase sales of its popular guitars.

But Gibson missed a key step in building its Internet strategy; it did not get the buy-in of its dealer network. When word of

Gibson's foray into online retailing hit the streets, its dealers went "ballistic," so much so that Gibson pulled the plug on its online guitar sales efforts. These days, gibson.com sells only music accessory items and refurbished guitars that are on consignment. The Web site points new guitar sales prospects to authorized Gibson dealerships.

The decision whether or not to disintermediate the traditional channel structure is a critical one that has consequences unique to each business. As with any new business strategy, the implication of the strategy execution needs to be examined and anticipated.

Distribution and sales chaos brought about by the Web isn't confined to its role in manufacturing customer relationships. There are many other permutations of chaos. Further down the food chain are distributors who are using the Web to build and retain dealer business. PC distributors, for example, are doing what they can to differentiate themselves in the highly competitive computer market by adding value to existing dealer programs via the Internet—offering new electronic commerce services such as technical support, catalogs, real-time order status, and electronic invoicing.

Disorder can also bring about new business opportunities. pcOrder, a provider of Internet-based electronic commerce solutions that enable the computer industry's suppliers, resellers, and end-users to buy and sell computer products online, is one such example. pcOrder has created a third-party electronic backbone that maintains data on over two hundred thousand computer products from over four thousand manufacturers. This data includes configuration-related technical specifications, pricing and availability, photographs of products, and marketing information. Its business model allows companies in the IT industry to leverage the Internet to bring new levels of efficiency to the distribution process without having to build costly, proprietary e-commerce catalog and ordering systems on their own. By aggregating, validating, and structuring this data, pcOrder provides a comprehensive e-commerce solution for the IT industry.

Fruit of the Loom is an example of a manufacturer that took an unusual approach to using the Web to strengthen its distributor relationships. The company's ActiveWear division developed a strategic initiative to utilize the Web to partner with distributors and resellers, thereby strengthening the distribution/reseller relationship rather than disintermediating it. The ActiveWear division manufactures and sells decorative clothing (fleecewear, sporty knit shirts, and T-shirts) that can be decorated with logos, pictures, and designs. ActiveWear sells the "plain wrap" products to fifty key distributors, who in turn sell the items to over thirty thousand resellers. Local designers and resellers, such as college bookstores or touring music show promoters, perform the decorative work and sell the customized items to consumers.

Decorative clothing is a regional business. Fruit of the Loom's distributors play a vital role in coordinating price, availability, product information, and order-tracking requests. Rather than circumventing its distributors by selling direct to resellers via the Web, ActiveWear thought it could better utilize the Web to improve its business relationships—empowering and streamlining its antiquated distribution system.

The company launched its ActiveWear Online system as part of a deliberate, twofold corporate business strategy. Its first goal was to improve loyalty among distributors and resellers. The company realized this first goal by creating a Web management system for ActiveWear clothing designers, resellers, and distributors that streamlined its production and fulfillment operations. Among other features, the new Web-based system allowed users to access sales data and inventory lists and to locate channel partners in their geographic area. The new system pleased ActiveWear's customers and saved the company money—reducing cycle time and lowering its inventory levels. Goal number two was to help its distributors set up their own Web sites by giving them servers prepackaged with inventory-management software, customized catalogs, and content templates that would help them offer productive Web sites to their subset of customers—which would in turn help participating distributors to differentiate themselves in the market. Distributors design and host their own sites, utilizing Fruit of the Loom page templates and logos as needed. Many of them also post information about competitors' products on their sites. If competing items are not in stock, however, Fruit's inventory-management software automatically recommends a comparable Fruit of the Loom selection.

For Fruit of the Loom, the results are impressive: increased profits, improved customer satisfaction, and improved efficiencies in organizational operations—such as shortened cycle times and lower order management costs.

Retailers have experienced their own version of chaos attempting to run an e-commerce operation while maintaining storefronts. Not only are there strategic conflicts, but tactical ones as well. One major electronics chain we know of decided to sell products online and to manage the Web site as another store. The change and investment has been substantial for this company, but it was mandatory. As its CIO said about the Web in a recent Cognitiative Pulse of the Customer focus group, "If you're not there, you're not there."

Rise of the New Intermediaries

New types of companies are emerging to offer commerce and content aggregation services designed to make the job of conducting business on the Web easier. While traditional intermediaries struggle to redefine their role in the value chain, new intermediaries are identifying opportunities and filling the new voids created by the Web.

Intermediary functions that benefit customers include assistance in search and evaluation of products and services, needs assessment and product matching, risk reduction, and product distribution/delivery. Intermediary functions that benefit site producers include creating and disseminating product information, creating product awareness, influencing consumer purchases, providing customer information, reducing exposure to risk, and reducing costs of distribution through transaction scale economies.

Does the classic middleman lose out to the new intermediary? The answer is yes and no. As discussed above, the Web is definitely eliminating many traditional middleman functions. The Web is also giving rise to new intermediaries who offer online buyers quick and efficient ways to find information, do comparative shopping, and purchase the goods and services they need.

Many complex transactions, such as purchasing a home, will continue to benefit from *both* skilled middlemen; in this case, for example, agents who help walk consumers through a very complex purchase decision cycle, and online intermediaries, such as iOwn.com (*www.iown.com*), who educate suspects and prospects and help turn them into bonafide customers for its partners. Many of these online agents are already offering valuable aggregation services in the fields of insurance, travel, books, music, and automobile sales. Traditional middlemen operating in almost every commodity-based business are at risk of being edged out by new Web emissaries.

So who are they? What roles do they play? What benefits do they offer? The remainder of this chapter covers different intermediaries that have emerged in the Web channel and the impact they're having on traditional selling models.

PORTALS

Portals are entry points to the Internet that provide customers with categorized "yellow pages" of information. Classic search engine companies have morphed into online destination sites. The most popular of these destinations—Yahoo!/GeoCities, Excite/At Home, Lycos, Hotbot, and AltaVista—offer one-click point of entry to news, commerce sites, weather reports, message boards, sports information, e-mail accounts, search engines, personal finance, and other informative content.

Advanced portals sites are rapidly building their brands by providing personalized and customized "niche experiences" to go along with their sophisticated yellow pages of content links. Disney's online destination, Go Network (*www.go.com*), integrates original content from Disney and ABC. America Online is branching out from its roots as a proprietary online service to become more of a Webcasting network. Even Amazon.com has transformed its online bookstore into a consumer commerce portal by diversifying its product line into videos, music, home furnishings, and specialty gift items.

More and more companies are getting into the portal business. In December 1998, Network Associates launched its "smart portal," called McAfee Online (*www.mcafee.com*). The site is designed as a one-stop PC support portal—a place for PC computer users to get the latest technology news, purchase and download Network Associate's software products, and even collaborate using hosted e-mail.

Netscape and AOL's Netcenter (*www.netcenter.com*) has revamped its online offerings in hopes of becoming the premier enterprise portal. Its "affinity portal" helps companies build Net center–powered destination sites that can also serve as corporate intranets. The affinity portal functions like a classic portal—offering search features, news headlines, stock quotes, Web search capabilities, and free e-mail—and includes company-specific content on the site.

Some portal sites are integrating "smartbots," "shopbots," or "intelligent agent" technology into their aggregation offerings to provide consumers with advanced comparison shopping choices. According to a definition found on the *www.whatis.com* Web site, an "intelligent agent" is simply a program that gathers information or performs some other service without a user's immediate presence and on some regular schedule. Typically, an agent program, using parameters you have provided, searches all or some part of the Internet, gathers information you're interested in, and presents it to you on a daily or other periodic basis.

In 1998, Amazon.com acquired one of the top intelligent agent aggregators—a company called Junglee. Junglee technology allows consumers to locate, compare, and transact millions of products across the Internet—instantly comparing price and availability of items for sale on most major consumer e-commerce sites. To some degree, companies like Amazon.com are threatened by agent technology, whose primary function is to streamline the shopping process—reducing consumer dependency on any one commerce portal. Amazon.com is experimenting with various ways to integrate Junglee's technology into the Amazon.com site experience.

Not to be outdone, Bertelsmann Ventures, the independent venture capital fund of media giant Bertelsmann Group, invested in Acses (*www.acses.com*), a German company whose online aggregation service is similar to the Junglee system. Acses is a leading comparison shopping service that utilizes proprietary technology to uniquely track the lowest prices on book titles sold over the Internet. Visitors using Acses simply choose any book, and the Internet software robot then automatically visits twenty-five Internet bookstores simultaneously to retrieve the current prices for the specific book from each store. Availability, shipping costs, and shipping times are taken into account as well. The system also offers an innovative shopping cart system, which allows users to find the best price for a whole set of multiple products and to fulfill the transaction with just a few clicks of the mouse.

VIRTUAL RETAILERS

The emergence of the Internet has created a new breed of electronic retailers that had never before existed in the offline world. Video and DVD retailer Reel.com (*www.reel.com*); Web grocery service firm Streamline, Inc. (*www.streamline.com*); online software superstore (*www.beyond.com*); and online investment service firm E*Trade are just a few examples. In addition, the innovations these companies introduced have led to new methods of managing inventory and logistics.

Some Internet retailers, such as Amazon.com, have streamlined their operations by creating complex sales and shipping procedures that allow the company to avoid costly inventories and pass that savings on to their customers. This type of on-demand inventory system gives virtual retailers a competitive advantage over their offline competitors—and that's one of the reasons so many traditional retail outlets are now launching their own online storefronts.

AGGREGATORS

The vast majority of the world's data exists outside the reach of the average person—scattered across Web sites, proprietary file systems, and legacy applications. Aggregators help make that data available and save customers time and effort by offering targeted information access and comparative-shopping search services on their Web sites. Examples include companies such as online insurance aggregator, InsWeb (*www.insweb.com*), and the homebuyer destination site, Realtor.com.

"There are distinct advantages to selling insurance over the Internet," claims Darrell Ticehurst of InsWeb. "The insurance industry is a series of complex products—and the complexity of those products has mystified a lot of people. With the Internet, we are able to empower the consumer by providing knowledge about what the insurance products really are."

The Internet empowers consumers to educate themselves and make their own decisions. Its ability to allow consumers to drill down to the details of a product or service—at their convenience—is one its myriad benefits. Consumers like the idea of not having to interface with high-pressure sales agents—especially when all they need is information. Insurance companies are embracing the Internet because they realize that they can reach a wider audience of potential customers, remove costs from the sales cycle, and improve customer satisfaction in one fell swoop.

Another example of a new type of intermediary is Web-based realtor information network, Realtor.com, which educates potential homebuyers and connects them with local real estate agents. Rather than eliminating the middleman, Realtor.com strengthens the real estate market by providing a crucial service—helping to produce potential buyers. This aggregation service benefits all involved parties—consumers get access to free information, middlemen get leads, and the parent company gets monetary compensation for providing the service.

Online automobile intermediaries such as autobytel.com (*www.autobytel.com*) have improved the car buying process by aggregating purchase requests from prospective customers to its network of dealers, who then call the prospect with a low, no-haggle price. Automobile dealers have embraced autobytel.com's Web intermediation service because dealers have found this approach saves a tremendous amount of what it traditionally costs to market, sell, and deliver a vehicle to a consumer.

According to executives at autobytel.com, it costs the average dealer just over $100,000 to sell one hundred cars through traditional means versus $20,000 through autobytel.com. This is because the quality of leads provided to dealers by autobytel.com has proven to be superior to leads gathered by salespeople through phone calls, or through other traditional sources.

Perhaps the most complex technical aspect to autobytel.com's business model is guaranteeing follow-through on the part of the dealer. When autobytel.com delivers a sales lead to a dealer, the dealer needs some sense of how qualified and interested that prospect is—so he can decide how much effort to put into the follow-up. By the same token, when autobytel.com delivers a sales lead, it depends on the dealer organization to follow up on that lead as promised. To ensure quality service, autobytel.com constantly monitors its dealer network to make sure that the dealers do indeed follow up—ensuring that autobytel.com meets the needs of its users. If a dealer doesn't follow up at an acceptable quality level, autobytel.com will take steps to replace that dealer. The dealer's level of responsiveness is critical to the success of autobytel.com's business, so it is setting higher standards for follow-ups. This is true of most online intermediaries.

Another example of an aggregator is Chemdex. In 1996, Chemdex (*www.chemdex.com*) launched an aggressive online business venture to dramatically improve the process of buying and selling life science products to the research and laboratory market. The Chemdex Web site contains over 250,000 product listings from over 120 suppliers. To do business with Chemdex, customers must be qualified users of biological and chemical reagents. New customers complete a registration form on Chemdex's Web site, and a response is guaranteed within twenty-four hours of submission. If a scientist establishes her own account with Chemdex, the only limit on her spending is that of her credit card or the amount of credit Chemdex has extended to her. If a company sets up an account for its scientists at Chemdex, the scientists may be subject to per-order and per-month spending limits. Scientists can check their spending limits at any time on the

"Your Profile" page of the site. If they exceed their organization's buying limits, Chemdex automatically routes the order to a designated approver. The approver receives an e-mail with the order details and may add notes, approve the order, or return the order to its originator.

David Perry of Chemdex explains it: "We're in the business of improving the process of buying and selling life science products. The only option our customers have had until now is to search through an average of forty catalogs on a shelf above their desk to find what they're looking for. If every one of those catalog suppliers puts up their own Web site, now the customer has to search through forty Web sites to find what they need. That's no easier than using a print catalog. It may be harder, actually. Chemdex is an aggregator—a one-stop shop. And suppliers understand that."

Chemdex serves three key constituents: the researcher, the enterprise, and the supplier. For the researcher, Chemdex has developed chemdex.com, a fully transactional, Web-based electronic catalog and ordering system for life science products, currently offering the world's single largest source of biological chemicals and reagents. Chemdex.com offers specialized search engines and transaction functionality, which reduce the time spent by scientists when procuring products and greatly increase the effectiveness of their purchasing by offering all the information necessary to make the best purchase decision.

For the enterprise, Chemdex has developed a suite of solutions that offer a range of purchasing management and systems integration functionality to complement chemdex.com. Through automated workflow approval processes, consolidated and automated invoicing and billing, and systems integration, these products bring cost reductions and more effective purchasing to the list of benefits provided to Chemdex customers.

In today's competitive world of life-science research and development (R&D), cost savings and streamlined processes are a strategic imperative for economic success. For life science product suppliers, Chemdex has developed a suite of solutions offering a range of supply-chain automation, reporting support, and direct marketing capabilities.

Chemdex is making waves in its marketplace. Its first enterprise purchasing customer, Genentech, Inc. (the world's top biotech firm), has fully implemented the Chemdex enterprise solution as a procurement front-end to order antibodies, enzymes, hormones, and other biotechnology products from suppliers. With Chemdex, Genentech's researchers, scientists, and lab technicians source, compare, and purchase biological and chemical reagents via the Genentech intranet, which links them to a customized Chemdex Web site. More than 240,000 products, from 80 percent of the leading biological and chemical reagent suppliers, are available for purchase through Chemdex—more than five times as many products as the most comprehensive catalog. The Chemdex Web interface incorporates Genentech's parameters for purchasing approvals, spending limits, and other procurement business rules.

The dynamic nature of the Chemdex system allows suppliers to publish an unlimited amount of product and technical information, providing Genentech researchers with the resources they need to make the best buying decision. Being able to access hundreds of thousands of products from thousands of suppliers using the specially developed Chemdex search engine greatly reduces the time necessary to complete a purchase.

AUCTIONEERS

Online auction sites help connect both consumer and business-to-business buyers to deep-discount, refurbished, or consignment items that they may not have had any way of accessing prior to the advent of the Web.

eBay (*www.ebay.com*) is a person-to-person Internet trading community in which users buy and sell personal items in an auction format. Individuals, rather than big businesses, use eBay to buy and sell items in more than one thousand categories, including collectibles, computers, toys, antiques, sports memorabilia, antique dolls, coins, stamps, magazines, music, books, glassware, photography, jewelry, and electronics.[6] eBay provides over 70,000 new items each day from which users may choose. Sellers are attracted to eBay as a destination site to conduct business because there are large numbers of sales prospects gathered in one place.

The auction format is fairly straightforward. Prospects browse and make bids on merchandise. If an item sells, eBay charges the seller a percentage of the closing price. eBay customers can also submit comments about their online auction experiences with sellers, using a satisfaction rating system. The system is based on each party's conduct during a transaction, and the scores are added to the seller's online profile.

Public online auctions such as eBay deal with the daily threat of fraudulent goods being offered for sale on their sites in much the same way as newspapers must contend with fraudulent classified advertising. To help reduce its liability and prevent fraud, eBay offers an escrow service to hold funds until goods are delivered. They also provide free buyers' insurance, and they prohibit sellers from bidding on their own merchandise.

ONSALE, Inc. (*www.onsale.com*) also operates online auctions, where it sells such items as refurbished and closeout computers, consumer electronics, and outdoor equipment. The company's "around-the-clock" auctions allow its one million registered bidders to bid on thousands of items each week. Perhaps most impressive is user enthusiasm for the service. Seventy-seven percent of its orders are from repeat customers.

ONSALE continues to broaden its product variety through strategic business alliances, resulting in more than one thousand other Web sites linking to the company's site. To offset the threat of any competitive offerings, ONSALE launched atCost, a destination on its Web site that offers brand name computer products at verified wholesale prices. Rather than looking at this new sales strategy as a huge moneymaker, the company says it will rely on advertising revenue and the fees it collects for service contracts and leases to provide it with a slim operating margin.

"One of the essential elements of our auction business model is that we can give better price recovery to our vendors than other alternative channels of distribution," says Barry Peters, marketing director of ONSALE. "And you could say that in some respects, we're a supply driven company, because the second we can get better price recovery for vendors, they will give us more supplies and, therefore, we can grow our business. But you can equally say that we're demand driven, because the way we get a higher price for the goods—and for the vendors—is to drive more demand. If you drill our business model down to its basic elements, it's finding the right balance between supply and demand."

Priceline.com Incorporated (*www.priceline.com*) puts a new twist on the e-commerce auction scheme by allowing its consumers to name their own prices for a variety of products and services, such as airline tickets, hotel rooms, and new cars. It's fundamentally a new way for buyers to negotiate prices and for suppliers to generate low cost sales. Visitors to the Web site name the price they want to pay for an item or service. Priceline.com's patented reverse auction system then communicates bids to companies willing to sell excess inventory at below-retail prices.

The company has invested heavily in promoting its brand through an aggressive "top-of-mind" brand building campaign, using radio, television, and print spots featuring William Shatner as its celebrity spokesperson. The company reports that it sold over seventy-five thousand airline tickets during its first six months of operation and claims it is now the fifth most-recognized Internet brand in America.

FreeMarkets OnLine (*www.freemarkets.com*) is an Internet-based, business-to-business reverse auction site where, instead of buyers deciding how much they'll pay, sellers determine how much they'll take. FreeMarkets dubs itself "the world's first online industrial market maker for custom industrial products." Sellers post what they need and how much they're willing to pay for it. FreeMarkets schedules an auction date and the duration of the auction period. Suppliers compete for business by submitting bids to the FreeMarkets Web site, using the company's proprietary BidWare® software (to ensure the security and privacy of the bidding process). The seller chooses the most attractive bid, and FreeMarkets closes the deal—earning a prenegotiated fee from the purchaser.

So far, the company's unique online business model is doing well—more than one thousand suppliers have submitted bids to FreeMarkets OnLine. The company has serviced Fortune 500 companies such as Caterpillar, Zenith, Procter and Gamble, United Technologies, and Zenith. Company revenues were reportedly $103 million in 1998 and are expected to climb to over $300 million for 1999.

How Are the New Intermediaries Making Money?

Business models for making money in the online space vary from company to company. Some companies (e.g., in the publishing industry) may believe more firmly in the subscription model; companies with a background in cable television or the gaming industry may prefer the pay-per-use (similar to pay-per-view) approach; while others rely on product sales margins, as in more traditional retailing. Many intermediaries are not committed to just one sales/business model and employ multiple strategies at the same time, similar to what AOL does.

"Ultimately, in AOL's case, success probably depends on the simultaneous exploitation of multiple business models," claims Internet analyst Paul Palumbo. "The company already employs flat rate pricing, sells advertising and sponsorships, rents retail space, exacts payment for carriage from content partners, has a commerce component, and packages its games in a premium area. It's the cable MSO model [Master Standing Offers]. AOL's case is very representative of the online business model question in general. The more inclusive of different media, the stronger the revenue streams have to be to cover production, licensing, hardware, bandwidth, and maintenance costs. The scarcities on the Internet are bandwidth and eyeballs, and AOL—and everybody else—must constantly recalculate how to pay for those necessary ingredients."

Here are a few examples of how Web intermediaries are making money:

TRANSACTION MODEL

Aggregators in this category, such as Yahoo! and 1-800-Flowers.com, receive fees for referring customers to manufacturers or fulfillers. Take 1-800-Flowers.com for example. The company's franchisees receive the same percentage of an order as any other florist-to-florist transaction. The sending florist (1-800-Flowers.com) receives 20 percent of the total price of the order; the wire service—the company that is the clearinghouse for the order (i.e., AFS, FTD, or TELEFLORA)—would receive 7 percent of the price; and the fulfilling florist receives 73 percent.[7] 1-800-Flowers.com also makes money through a service charge that is added to the customer bill (along with sales tax or shipping fees). The service charge as of early 1999 varied from $5.99 to $15.99, depending on the price of the order.

When an online book retailer uses a portal, such as Yahoo! or Excite, in order to facilitate a "click-thru" that eventually leads to a sale, the book retailer often pays the portal a "finder's fee" or "transaction fee," which can vary from a few cents to several dollars. That's well below the cost to acquire a new customer using traditional marketing channels. One can see why companies pay the advertising fees charged by the portals—it's an economically sound business deal for the online retailer. It's a much less expensive option than acquiring new customers through other means, such as print advertising.

"It costs us $100 to acquire a new account today—it used to be $40 five years ago," says Joseph Tripodi, executive vice president, global marketing, Mastercard International. "My sense is that the Internet will, at a minimum, help reduce some of these costs."[8]

RESELLER MODEL

Online intermediaries, such as Egghead.com, Cyberian Outpost, Chemdex, eToys, PC Mall, and Webshopper.com, generate revenue just like traditional, offline retail stores. Resellers buy products at wholesale prices and mark up the items for sale. Reseller margins range from 30 to 50 percent of the price per order. Many of these sales are made possible by aggressive manufacturers, who are helping to increase sales by pointing customers directly to resellers' doorsteps.

Software leader Symantec is a good example of a company doing just that. To get a hotlink from the Symantec store, a reseller has to create a Symantec buypage or Symantec boutique on its Web site that will take customers directly to a buy destination. Resellers don't pay a fee for this service. They just have to build a Symantec boutique—according to a preset template or standards—then Symantec hooks them up. Currently, Symantec is not in the business of taking a percentage from each sale when it transfers a customer, but, of course, it earns revenue every time a product sells—whoever sells it.

Chemdex Corporation takes the supplier's product information, reformats it, and places it into its own database. Then a Web front-end allows customers to access that database to conduct searches for the items they're looking for. When an order is placed with Chemdex, the company forwards that order to the supplier, who is responsible for shipping the item directly to the customer. The money comes through Chemdex, which takes its cut (10 to 15 percent of the purchase price) and then passes the remaining monies on to the supplier.

THE ADVERTISING MODEL

For some types of Web sites, advertising is a critical revenue stream. For others, advertising revenues are irrelevant. The portal sites are examples of sites for which the advertising revenue stream is very important. Advertisers on portal sites are usually companies that want users to click on their ads, which often take the user to the advertiser's site or to a special area of the portal site. Advertisers pay for the portal customer's "eyeballs," similar in concept to television advertising. Advertising fees are generally based on the number of "click-thrus," which is a type of performance model.

The jury is still out on whether or not this is an effective way to advertise and whether advertising on the Internet will generate significant revenue for other online business ventures beyond high-traffic, high-volume sites. Some research has shown that banner ads are more effective in consumer markets than in business-to-business markets.

"Banner ads have not worked for us," claims Dell's Langer. "We're not yet convinced that banner advertising is a good place to put our dollars. When we do set up a banner ad agreement, we only do it on a "click-thru" basis or a pay-per-lead basis."

As in any type of advertising, vehicles that deliver targeted, screened eyeballs are more effective than less focused means. Specialty Web commerce sites that deliver well-qualified eyeballs are increasingly earning healthy advertising revenues as a result.

Companies who have advertised on Preview Travel's site have found that access to a commerce-ready consumer has yielded results, or "click-thrus," of at least double what they experience on more generic Web sites, according to Preview Travel. In fact, in the fourth quarter of fiscal year 1998, results showed that Preview Travel experienced a 3–5 percent "click-thru" rate as compared with industry-average "click-thru" rates of 1–1.5 percent.

Subscription Model

Subscription models, where customers pay an ongoing right-to-use fee, are key for certain types of Web site situations. Online gaming sites have discovered that monthly flatrate pricing models are effective. Ten Entertainment Network (*www.ten.net*) offers a flat-rate plan at $19.95 per month for unlimited use of its service. To subscribe to the *Wall Street Journal* Interactive Edition (*www.wsj.com*), an annual subscription costs $29 with proof of a print subscription to any edition of the *Wall Street Journal* or *Barron's,* and $59 for nonprint subscribers.

Subscriptions also come in the form of a site license—where an information company charges an organization a flat monthly or yearly fee for group access to the proprietary information. A law firm that pays for multiple employee access to an online trademark database, for example, might first have to purchase a group site license prior to gaining access to the data.

The subscription service model is the preferred moneymaking model for many online businesses for a number of reasons.

It's easier to manage accounts, it's more convenient for customers, and it encourages repeat use because customers are not worried about spending too much money. The drawback, of course, is that the subscription model places a cap on per-customer earnings. It can also invite high-volume site traffic, as the user is not concerned about running up his bills—and therefore is not motivated to disconnect or curtail his onsite activities.

PAY-PER-USE MODEL

This is the classic "pay-as-you-go" model, which charges users for limited use of a product or service. Pay-per-view movie services charge for the right to watch one playing of a movie via satellite or cable. Some online information services, such as Paul Kagan and Associates' Baseline (*www.pkbaseline.com*), a service that supplies film reviews, box office statistics, archived entertainment news, and talent credits, charges its customers for each information report a user downloads. Prices range from $.95 to $49.95 per document. The company also offers subscriptions to Baseline.

Some companies' products or services have such a low price point that using a credit card for each transaction doesn't make sense. For example, instead of charging individually for every card purchased, many online greeting card companies charge fees of under ten dollars to a customer's credit card, then debit that prepaid balance from fifty cents to one dollar every time an electronic card is sent to someone. As a business model, one has to question whether or not such small transaction fees are worth the effort. How many five-dollar orders does a firm have to generate before earning a profit? Perhaps the strongest argument in favor of such a model is that the low buy-in price encourages more people to use the service.

LICENSE FEE MODEL

A basic license fee results when a company pays to be part of an aggregator's referral network. For instance, an insurance carrier might pay an aggregator like InsWeb an annual license fee to be one of the recommended insurance carriers on the InsWeb site.

To join autobytel.com's network of dealers, car dealers pay anywhere from $1,500 to $2,500 per month. By late 1998, autobytel.com's North American Network had signed up over four thousand accredited dealers, who paid this license fee to be part of the company's growing automobile referral network.

Hybrid Model

In reality, what's more common among the leading Web companies is a hybrid approach to generating revenue online. Barry Diller, CEO of USA Networks, says, "No successful business will be based solely on advertising revenues. Companies must provide services and transactions and focus on the total customer experience."[9]

For example, online real estate portal Realtor.com claims that it has three unique revenue streams: subscriptions, publishing, and transactions.

In the subscription revenue arena, Realtor.com sells personalized home pages to 720,000 licensed realtors throughout the United States, charging them three hundred dollars and up for the service. Publishing revenue, its second revenue stream, splits into three areas: ad revenue, microsite sponsorships, and content delivery. Ad revenue is generated by charging businesses a fee to post banner ads on a site. The second area, a microsite sponsorship, occurs when a company, such as The Home Depot, pays a fee to take ownership of a specific content area on the Realtor.com site—like the home improvement section. The Home Depot brands this area with its corporate logo and provides additional value by adding unique content to it. To generate revenue for content delivery, Realtor.com licenses certain content areas of its site—such as Real Times real estate news service—to large firms, such as Coldwell Banker, who use this content to add value to their own corporate sites. The third area is transaction revenue: For example, in the coming months and years, Realtor.com plans to charge for real estate related services such as access to credit reports and online mortgage applications and approvals.

Conclusion

The number of customers who want to buy online is increasing. Businesses want to remove inefficiencies from current business processes. The Web is empowering both groups to fulfill these goals.

If all indications are correct, the Web is more than simply a marketing channel. Many firms are utilizing the Web as a direct sales vehicle to reach out to prospects and customers. It's an especially valuable channel strategy for those companies who previously had no choice but to sell through traditional channels. The Web eliminates the frustratingly inefficient process of presenting a product and hoping that a reseller is skilled and interested enough to sell it.

Electronic commerce is just beginning to scratch the surface of what is possible. Nobody knows for sure exactly how the traditional sales process or the channel pipelines will ultimately be impacted by the Web. What we do know is that by circumventing traditional retailers, agents, and brokers via the Web, customers save time and money, and they are empowered to bypass dysfunctional sales and communication processes that they would rather avoid.

The stranglehold that current sales, marketing, and distribution strategies have on businesses will eventually fail them. Many companies are contemplating whether they should sell their products and services online—and quite a few of them are struggling with the issue of channel conflict. Many fear a backlash from their retail distributors or salespeople if they commit to any bold online initiatives. But forward-thinking business leaders know that they must develop workarounds that empower their customers, bring down costs, and increase sales.

Chapter Four

Develop Your Brand in the Web Context

"We are entering a phase on the Internet where brand muscle will be the determinant of success."

—Tom Melcher, Senior Vice President, Strategy and
Business Development, C/NET

The concept of "brand" can be defined as using a name, symbol, design, term, or some combination thereof in order to identify a service, product, or company. Many traditional brands have come to connote the psychological connection between a product image and someone the buyer aspires to be, such as with automobiles, sporting goods, and designer clothing. While the intent of branding in the Web context is fundamentally the same, what constitutes a brand and how branding is achieved are different.

The level to which a Web experience meets the needs and expectations of visitors plays a crucial role in establishing and maintaining brand loyalty. The more reliant your customers become on using the Web to conduct business with you, the more their impressions of your brand are based on the experience that your site offers. As more facets of the Consumption Cycle—shopping, buying, receiving, and consuming—move to the Web, customer exposure to vendor marketing and communications efforts becomes more Web-oriented. Customer modes of behavior and interaction with vendors begin to change—customers don't go to physical stores as often, they don't need sales presentations to know what to reorder, and they read more online publications and are therefore less exposed to print advertising. As this trend progresses, the Web becomes the locus of the vendor-customer relationship.

Customers are coming to expect empowerment; they seek the ability to perform all steps within the Consumption Cycle online. Whether or not you effectively enable that kind of experience can make the difference between brand loyalty and brand rejection. A brand on the Web is not really about a psychological connection between a product image and someone the buyer aspires to be, as it is with traditional branding. It's about enabling customers to successfully and consistently meet their specific needs through an online experience that is productive and satisfying.

What's Different When the Web is the Vehicle?

People who visit a Web site still engage in a purchasing process—becoming aware, making a buying decision, using the item, evaluating the decision, etc. What's different in the Web world is that the customer controls the sequence in which marketing events and messages for developing brand are experienced. That requires a different strategy for "air cover" and visibility to drive traffic to your site, and for a different type of interaction once a visitor gets there. With the customer much more in control, targeted marketing becomes dependent on being able to track customers' online behavior to understand and address their interests and needs. If properly executed, this can be a powerful tool. For instance, on-the-fly promotions can be offered to a customer based on assumptions made from tracking her onsite behavior, potentially leading to increased purchasing. But the trick is transforming those kinds of experiences into sustained brand preference and loyalty. In the Web marketplace, information on pricing, cost bases, and other comparative information is readily available, making customers sophisticated and savvy shoppers. When the customer is armed with such information, brand loyalty plays a diminished role in purchase decisions. This phenomenon was predicted by leading economist Robert Kuttner in a May 1998 *BusinessWeek* column: "The Internet is a nearly perfect market because information is instantaneous and buyers can compare the offerings of sellers worldwide. The result is fierce price competition, dwindling product differentiation, and vanishing brand loyalty. Imitators, especially those with deep pockets, can steal innovations as fast as they are invented and marketed."[1]

What this inevitably means is that more products become commodities—the best scenario for online purchasing from the customer's point of view. But for the vendor, this means the criteria for brand preference changes. As purchasers look more and more to sites that are the easiest and most satisfactory places to shop, differentiation based on price and channel gets eliminated, leveling the playing field. Provided the ultimate quality of the purchased goods is satisfactory, the key brand differentiator then will be the site experience.

THE SITE MUST ENABLE THE CONSUMPTION CYCLE

Most companies still use traditional marketing communications methods today to promote their Web business. While these methods can be useful in raising awareness and bringing traffic to the site, the site itself bears the burden of engaging visitors, converting them into customers, and encouraging return visits and purchases. If you focus in on the marketing part of the equation, a Web site must transform a visitor from "mildly aware" to "somewhat interested" to "truly considering" to "really evaluating whether they should buy" to "making the decision." That's a big responsibility for one medium.

Some companies are working to migrate a large proportion of their customers to online relationships. Not everyone will elect to make an actual purchase online. Indeed, some goods may not be suitable to sell via this channel. But the site, as a marketing vehicle, must still encourage and facilitate the purchase process.

For example, a customer might choose to gather information online, but the purchase may go through an offline channel—for example, via telephone or at a retail store. In fact, some sites are designed to educate the prospective customer but then direct him or her to another channel to consummate the sale. Wherever the sales actually occurs, the role that the site experience plays in leading up to the sale is key to establishing brand preference.

Branding Activities in the Web World

If branding for the Web is different, then the activities in the branding process—from visibility to awareness to preference to loyalty—must adapt for a new medium. Awareness will be generated through new kinds of marketing activities, requiring additional or reapportioned marketing budgets. A Web site must effectively deliver on a company's traditional brand perceptions and value propositions, prompting some examination of what those truly are from the perspective of its market and customer base. And, as these new activities are introduced, they must be designed and deployed to coexist with existing business strategies. In this section, we'll look at how these new activities should be viewed and integrated into traditional branding processes.

BUILDING BRAND AWARENESS REQUIRES SIGNIFICANT INVESTMENTS IN MULTIPLE MARKETING DISCIPLINES

Traditional branding involves multiple marketing activities, such as various forms of advertising and promotion, to create brand awareness. Brand preference extends from customers identifying with a particular brand's image and a related positive association, such as receiving consistent quality in a grocery item or looking a certain way in a given designer's jeans. Billions of dollars are spent annually on marketing activities to capture customer attention and, hopefully, loyalty.

Web branding must go a step beyond. Activities from the traditional marketing mix must still be carried out, but now with a new or additional call to action: Go visit my Web site. Campaigns from advertising to direct mail now always include an invitation to visit the sponsor's site. URLs (Web addresses) can be found on everything from clothing tags to cereal boxes. So, along with traditional marketing expenditures, online companies must now also execute new Web marketing programs to cultivate a demand for their online offerings. New Web marketing mechanisms, like banner advertising and portal anchor tenancy, have evolved at lightning speed and must now be considered in the marketing mix. Other vehicles, such as search engines, have also become intrinsic to awareness and lead generation. And since the site *experience* becomes the brand in the customer's mind, that experience must be positive when the visitor finally gets there.

Obviously, this can all be an expensive proposition. While most companies have at least a modest marketing budget, you now need to increase or readjust marketing allocations to fund a mix of both offline and online initiatives to establish and strengthen your Web brand. This can include not only marketing programs, but new staff positions and/or the retraining of existing staff as well. These new budget items may well mean that trade-offs in other company spending must be made, so investment options should be carefully analyzed.

Be sure to clearly define your marketing goals: Are you trying to attract people who are already on the Web, or are you targeting first-time users? Which existing marketed expenditures can be leveraged or refocused to help achieve Web strategy goals? Are you using the site to acquire new customers? Retain existing customers? Both? The relative weight of these objectives should have significant impact on where you decide to put resources. You should also take into account what other players in your market are spending and what it will take to rise above the noise level.

Let's consider how leading Internet-focused companies are approaching marketing and branding investments. Companies such as eBay, eToys, Priceline.com, Amazon.com, E*Trade, Excite, and Yahoo (all of whom have become household names) began setting the pace for a Web-inclusive marketing mix in 1998—proving true the dictum that, "You have to spend money to make money." Just how much are these kinds of companies spending?

An online advertising report by Cowles/Simba Information, a unit of Cowles Business Media, projected that online advertising spending would climb to more than $500 million in 1998 and $2.57 billion by 2000. Jupiter Communications, a New York communications research group, claims that Internet-focused companies will spend more than $7.7 billion in 2002, promoting their brands through a mix of print, broadcast, and online advertising. Traditional media is extremely expensive. A thirty-second commercial broadcast during a popular prime-time television show, for example, can cost $250,000 to $450,000. One thirty-second ad aired during the Super Bowl can cost over $500,000. Add to an "e-marketing" campaign expenditures like banner and portal ads, and you have a much larger investment.

It is clear that this is quickly adding up to some huge dollar amounts. Why the aggressive spending? Leading Internet-focused companies are trying to compress into two or three years what some companies have taken decades to establish. They are aggressively spending to reach profitability because they know that establishing brand presence, preference, and loyalty is absolutely critical to reaching the sales volumes required to make a Web site profitable. Their investors' expectations are set accordingly—midterm success is measured in volume growth, not profitability. While not all companies will be spending at these levels, it is important to note that these kinds of commitments and efforts have produced the more successful (and certainly visible) Web brands so far.

It can be valuable to determine what influences Web site visitors to frequent certain sites. In Cognitiative's Pulse of the Customer research, we routinely ask Web users how they learn about the Web sites they frequent so that we can keep an ongoing pulse on what marketing communications vehicles are most effective in raising awareness and driving traffic to Web sites. The two key influences consistently mentioned are articles in the press and references from friends. People perceive these two sources as most credible. They assume that information published by the press must be true. Similarly, people are most comfortable with references from other people they trust, which is why word of mouth referral is so important. Of course, experienced market researchers know that people don't always reliably remember all the marketing vehicles that ultimately influenced their behavior. People tend to remember the last thing that happened before going to a site, so you can't base marketing vehicle expenditure decisions solely on what Web users recall.

PORTALS

For companies targeting online consumers—such as America Online (AOL), where customers rely on a portal to organize their Web visits—a portal anchor tenancy deal can be a strategic branding option. This practice involves a company's paid, contractual relationship with a portal company, such as AOL, Excite, or Yahoo! in order to become an exclusive vendor on a portal site for a function-specific area. For example, Preview Travel is the exclusive provider of travel services on AOL and AOL.com.

Portal anchor tenancy is a high stakes game. Some companies are gambling that doing multimillion-dollar portal deals will lead to stronger brand awareness and customer acquisition, a theory that has yet to be fully proven due to the infancy of the practice. It's not uncommon to see $7–$10 million-a-year deals with the major portals, such as what occurred in 1998 with E*Trade. E*Trade Group, Inc. expanded its marketing and commerce agreements by striking deals with leading portal Yahoo! and ZDNet, Ziff-Davis's Internet destination site. The Yahoo! deal involves advertising, sponsorship, and promotional programs throughout the site. Finance and related areas of the Yahoo! network of properties, as well as a number of unique and targeted marketing and promotional programs created for E*Trade, were designed to directly reach the millions of Yahoo! Finance registered users.[2] The company's agreement with ZDNet calls for E*Trade to be the exclusive provider of online investment tools, including a portfolio manager and E*Trade's stock market game, to ZDNet's customer base.

To support its portal branding efforts, E*Trade unveiled an array of television, radio, newspaper, and magazine ads aimed to tap into the millions of financially sophisticated consumers who use the Web for investment research but who do not have trading accounts on the Internet.

One of the questions about the value of portal anchor tenancy or even portal site banner advertising is how to define their usefulness in terms of acquiring new customers. Once customers become Web savvy, their use of portals and their selection of which portal sites to frequent can change. Some users tend to develop favorite sites. Some prefer the convenience of going to one place to get the bulk of the online information they need, while others prefer a broader picture, accessing multiple sites. For convenience, some default to a portal offered by their Internet service provider (ISP). The choice of portals can also vary by the technical sophistication of the user and his level of comfort in selecting and customizing sites to deliver the content he is seeking. A user of AOL may have a very different profile than a user of CNet. Just as with traditional magazine advertising, portal companies should provide prospective tenants with thorough site statistics, such as traffic patterns and number of impressions, to facilitate this marketing investment decision.

Banner advertising on portals and other online destinations requires a smaller investment, but it is still risky. Cognitiative's focus group research indicates that, while banner advertising can be effective among home consumers, business consumers say that they do not click on banner advertising unless it is promoting something for which they are actively shopping. One focus group participant—an IT manager at a technology company—bluntly stated, "Banner ads usually lead you down an unproductive path. I don't have time to follow an ad around. I've got work to do."

For most companies, a mix of traditional and online expenditures is the right solution. Most are now realizing that the best approach is to integrate their marketing and mixed-media campaigns into one cross-media solution, where the strategic message is "authored" or "branded" once and incorporated into both traditional (print, direct marketing, video) and electronic (Web, Intranet, e-mail) vehicles to reach the broadest number of targeted customers.

"One of the key things about the Web is that it really complements the brick and mortar of life," says Roberts of Symantec. "The Web is completely fluid and changing all the time. I believe an organization must reflect that as well. Your overall strategy is represented in the direct mail pieces you do and the white papers you produce and the advertisements you run *and* your Web site. It should be a cohesive string. We work on a series of initiatives every year, and our Web site complements everything we are doing everywhere else."

YOUR VALUE PROPOSITION MUST DELIVER THE BRAND PROMISE

There are many companies whose Web presence is woefully disconnected from their value proposition in the offline world. Why is that? The Web has evolved so quickly that many organizations haven't fully considered or internalized how to transform their value proposition for it. This is not an easy thing to do. Companies need to clearly understand what their brand signifies in their market space and then determine how to meaningfully translate and consistently deliver that brand promise through a Web site experience. A company's reputation combined with the campaigns it implements to drive traffic to its site will set expectations. But poor execution can not only harm your Web presence—it can also backlash into your overall corporation position and perception.

Federal Express is a good example of a company that delivers well on its traditional brand promise in the online space. FedEx knows the reasons why customers prefer its service over other companies in the offline world—namely, delivery speed and package tracking. Consequently, they extend that competitive advantage online by empowering customers to instantly track packages. By providing this functionality online, FedEx raised the industry bar and forced its competitors to provide comparable services. On the Web, FedEx enjoys instant and credible brand recognition. In fact, FedEx's online presence may be serving to improve and strengthen brand image, as the site is much more empowering to its customers than its offline value proposition.

Its strong traditional brand, which is associated with quality performance, is a positive symbol for customers and prospects who
extend a level of trust to "e-FedEx," as long as that online experience meets the same level of quality that they are used to receiving from the offline FedEx.

On the other hand, advertising can raise an expected brand
promise that a Web site experience then does not deliver. In 1998,
automotive manufacturer Saturn launched a television advertising campaign that implied that a person could go to the Saturn
site, order a custom-configured car, and have that car delivered
to her door. The site, however, did not come through on that
promise—in fact, you could not order a car on Saturn's Web site
at all. On the site, shoppers were instructed to visit a nearby
Saturn dealer to make their purchase. Why did Saturn spend
millions of dollars on an ad campaign that made a promise it
couldn't fulfill? Probably because the company was focusing on
the "get it the way you want it, no hassles" aspect of their overall
positioning and didn't consider what its Web-focused advertising
was really implying.

While statistics on this campaign's effectiveness are not publicly available, we believe that the company ultimately lost credi-
bility among people who saw the TV ads and went to the Saturn
site with an incorrect expectation. The lesson? Take time to
research and understand your brand's existing reputation in
your market space and the marketing messages you've used to
convey it—then carefully translate this to the Web experience
you deliver.

BRAND CONTINUITY REQUIRES SMOOTH COEXISTENCE AMONG BUSINESS STRATEGIES

Grappling with existing business strategies has caused many
companies to be late to market with an effective Web presence,
as discussed in chapter 3. Other companies have misfired on
their first market entry, then struggled to find a better model.

For example, Macy's has evolved from a brochureware marketing site to an unsuccessful commerce site to an actual cyber-
store with a separate organization and mission. Macy's is faced

with the challenge of how to fulfill its traditional brand promise of making a wide array of products available, but now in the online environment. To achieve this, it must identify and reconcile strategic differences and conflicts involving pricing, promotions, merchandising, inventory management, and attracting people to the site. The challenge is amplified by the brand concerns of Macy's merchandise suppliers, who are also struggling with how to deliver their own brand promises online. For instance, Levi Strauss made a strategic decision to not allow Macy's to sell its products online, because Levi had launched Web sites of its own for both its Dockers and Levi's brands. Levi Strauss had a strong sense of how it wanted its brand promise represented in cyberspace, and it felt only Levi Strauss could do that well.[3] The company didn't trust Macy's to deliver its brand experience online. Kevin McSpadden, senior marketing manager for Dockers, is quoted as saying, "We want to present the brand the way we want our customers to interpret it online."[4]

This strategic channel decision forced Levi Strauss and Macy's, each with strong brands in its own right, to modify a long established business relationship and alter the market's expectations associated with their brands—namely, that Levi Strauss's clothing was readily available at Macy's.

As more companies enter the online marketplace, the interrelationships among many business practices—from pricing and discounting policies to alliances to product availability—must be carefully analyzed for their roles in the delivery of the overall corporate brand promise, then retained or replaced while keeping that brand promise intact.

Brand Loyalty Comes from Developing Trusted Relationships between Vendor and Customer

These days, trust is not just about credit card security. It's about delivering what you promise—repeatedly delivering a good experience. E-greetings' Levitan says, "Trust is built from the overall experience. And the experience includes service. If customers have a lousy experience, they will never buy anything from a Web site."

What elements of the experience impact trust? In the absence of human warmth and eye contact, Web visitors base their feelings of trust on how business processes are executed. Basic operational fundamentals become critical. Deliver what you say when you say you will deliver it. Give accurate information. Honestly report inventory levels. Make accurate and true claims about your company and your product capabilities.

Companies who don't follow these practices, whether intentionally or not, break down trust among those who have given them a chance. Delivering a trusted experience can be a very complex task, requiring sophisticated operational infrastructure. But the absence of well-executed business processes can dramatically deteriorate trust and erode brand loyalty.

Brand Preference Comes from a Successful Experience

The result of our observations is the fact that the quality of the online experience becomes what shapes brand preference. The experience and the brand are inextricably linked. The *experience* is the brand.

Lasting relationships are created by helping customers find what they want, facilitating the purchase transaction, providing post-purchase support, and doing all of these things really well. That's a tall order—and it gets harder every day because Web-savvy customers get increasingly more demanding. As Alan Fisher of ONSALE puts it, "The bar keeps getting raised by the customer."

In chapter 6, we'll look at some of the underlying technology issues that impact user experience in terms of time, productivity, user friendliness, personalization, and even entertainment value. But along with the technical infrastructure, a cross-organizational effort is essential to providing relevant, timely information, proactive incentives, reliable processes, and quality customer service, all of which contribute to the delivery of a satisfactory site experience and brand association.

Interestingly, for some companies, experience has always been the key success ingredient, long before the Web had even been thought of. In his book *Selling the Invisible,* Harry Beckwith observes the food industry: "People in the fast-food business used to think they were selling food. Then McDonalds came along and figured out that people weren't buying hamburgers. People were buying an experience."[5] The same holds true for the entertainment industry and even certain segments of the travel industry, such as luxury cruise ships, where the goal is not transportation from point to point. From a Web perspective, building brand loyalty starts with the homepage experience. Amazon's Jeff Bezos is quoted as saying that Amazon's focus is on creating a customer experience that is superior and sustainable. That's the essence of the Amazon brand. As Bezos says, "We will stay focused on the customer experience: selection, ease-of-use, price, and service. That's what we've done so far, and that's why the gap between us and our nearest competitor continues to grow."[6]

The Web Effect on branding is about creating an experience that satisfies the needs and wants of your customer better than any available alternative. Companies who can figure out how to use the Web to offer compelling online experiences that deliver what visitors and customers demand will be those who enjoy noticeable results in customer loyalty.

As we strive to better understand the phenomenon of customer loyalty and branding in the online arena, it is helpful to study real-world examples of companies who are battling for market share on a daily basis. Two such companies going head-to-head in the trading and brokerage field are Charles Schwab and E*Trade.

Branding Wars: Charles Schwab versus E*Trade

The emergence of online discount stock brokerages has been one of the most explosive business applications on the Web. Competition is fierce, as consumers are now much more empowered to demand lower brokerage fees and almost instantaneous trading. Two brokers have emerged as leading players in this market—Charles Schwab and Co. and E*Trade. These two companies provide an archetypal example of branding for the Web space, each approaching the task from a different position. Schwab had the challenge of extending its strong brand equity as the leading discount broker worldwide into a successful Web experience. E*Trade had to develop a completely new brand, which was born out of and focused exclusively at the online market.

Schwab began working on a robust online trading site back in 1995 as an add-on to its information-only site, *www.schwab.com*. It needed a site that securely and profitably enabled trading transactions and that could extend its popular, well-established brand onto the Internet. The goal was to create a premier online destination with top-quality information services and to develop intelligent alliances to help leverage and grow the brand.

The strategy included multiple initiatives. Schwab launched aggressive online banner ad campaigns, while at the same time it cut trading commissions to create barriers for the competition and garner positive PR. One phase of the advertising campaign was an international banner ad campaign developed with interactive agency Thunder House. In conjunction with Schwab's traditional media campaign developed by the McCann Erickson agency, Thunder House representatives developed online initiatives that mirrored the look and feel of McCann's print ads. They emphasized the benefits of online investing with Schwab Worldwide with the goal of establishing Schwab as the international market leader. This campaign was highly successful in reinforcing Schwab's branding message and in developing new leads for the firm. Other phases in the overall campaign even suggested that through online trading, Schwab would help its customers evolve into more sophisticated investors.

In addition to advertising, Schwab moved to gain visibility from other leading Web companies by developing strategic business alliances. It entered into agreements with both Intuit and Excite to offer investment education on Excite's Money and Investing Channel, programmed by Intuit's Quicken.com.

Schwab also worked to extend its very positive brand reputation to the online space through delivering a comprehensive series of services. The Schwab.com site offered top educational, research, and empowerment services, including high-quality research from leading market analysts, tools to help customers easily track historical performance of their mutual fund and equity holdings, and an electronic gateway to more than eighty third-party financial information providers. The site also offered daily news feeds and links to numerous investment data resources. These kinds of programs meet and often exceed the level of service traditionally provided by Schwab, enhancing the brand through the Web experience.

Combine this with an aggressive branding campaign, and average commissions reduced by more than half, and the result has been phenomenal success for Schwab. As of early 1999, *www.schwab.com* maintains over 2 million active online accounts holding over $145 billion in assets—and that number grows daily. With over $4 billion in securities trades per week, Schwab.com projects online trades will account for between 80 and 90 percent of its total trades by the year 2000—making it one of the largest e-commerce sites in the world.

E*Trade Group, Inc. had a different challenge. Aggressively entering the burgeoning online stock trading market, E*Trade had to quickly establish itself as an innovator and leader in this new space before others like Schwab could try to take ownership. Due to its pioneering practices and good execution, E*Trade actually reached quarterly profitability fairly early on. However, in 1998, E*Trade decided that longterm profitability in the online space would be the result of the depth and breadth of its brand. So rather than harvesting short-term profits, the company decided instead to invest its money into a massive brand-building campaign—an amalgam of carefully crafted strategic business alliances mixed with targeted advertising. In September 1998, E*Trade launched a $100 million, twelve-month advertising campaign. Without revealing exact percentages, Lisa Nash, vice president of customer management at E*Trade, says that, "substantially the largest chunk" of the company's ad dollars are being spent on the Internet versus traditional print and television advertising.

E*Trade pulled out all the stops when it invested in both online and offline advertising initiatives to rapidly build its brand. E*Trade's advertising campaign was aggressive, targeting both early online adopters and mainstream traders who had little or no experience logging onto the Web. Full-page print ads ran in leading newspapers, banner ads appeared for those browsing portals, and radio spots were featured in multiple markets. According to company press releases, the E*Trade marketing and advertising campaign has brought about measurable increases in brand awareness, including significant growth in new, active customer accounts and members. The company says it has added 132,000 active customer accounts during the first fiscal quarter of 1999, which ended on 31 December 1998—representing a 55 percent increase from the previous quarter's 85,000 new active accounts. Total accounts, which number 676,000, are up 109 percent from a year ago. In addition, E*Trade attracted 390,000 new members to its site last quarter, bringing the number of visitors that became members to more than 500,000 since E*Trade launched its public destination Web site in September 1998.

The effectiveness of E*Trade's marketing and advertising strategy also has been showcased in a report by NFO Worldwide, a global provider of marketing information. The report states that E*Trade had the single largest top-of-mind awareness of any online investing service, including Charles Schwab. In addition, according to MediaMetrics, E*Trade's "reach" during the first fiscal quarter of 1999; in other words, the number of people who accessed the site, was greater than the combined reach of Charles Schwab and Ameritrade.

It's interesting to note that while monitoring the return on its branding activities, Charles Schwab and Co. chose to step back from portals and focus on its own branding efforts. It already had a strong brand and decided that its marketing dollars were better spent on other vehicles like print and television advertising. E*Trade, on the other hand, focused strongly on Web branding channels. It aggressively pursued business partnerships with leading portal companies America Online, Microsoft Investor, CompuServe, WebTV, Prodigy Internet, and

Yahoo! to escalate brand visibility and awareness via these high-traffic sites.

Since Schwab is a larger company with larger traditional and online customer bases, it's impressive that a small start-up could rise in such a short amount of time to be a formidable competitor to a longtime market leader. We believe that much of the success enjoyed by both companies can be attributed to successful brand-awareness efforts, which translate into successful online customer experiences.

Appoint Empowered Executive Leadership and Create Organizational Structures that Work in a Web-Involved Company

"Whether to 'Webify' the company or not is similar to the question many CEOs were faced with two decades ago when deciding whether or not to computerize their companies. Look back with twenty years' hindsight at the introduction of personal computers as a strategic business vehicle. Is there a CEO who doesn't wish they had computerized much earlier than they actually did?"

—Anthony Sanchez, Senior Manager, Internet Programs and Development, Oracle Support Services

We began this book with a discussion of how Web-related issues need to be addressed quickly, efficiently, and at the highest levels within an organization. Now we narrow our scope to focus on how the structure of an organization is thrown into chaos when the Web becomes a primary business vehicle for a company. In this chapter we explore the leadership, organizational skills sets, and budgetary issues that occur when adopting the Web as a strategic business vehicle.

Every company that is in business today must determine how to adopt the Web as a vehicle while still maintaining the best business processes it already has. As discussed in chapter 3, it is interesting to ask how a company handles disintermediation without destroying a profitable distribution pipeline. How can employees be made to take on new Web responsibilities without taking away from the rest of their tasks? How can companies afford to invest in automating customer support via the Web when they still need employees to answer phone calls while the transformation is under way?

In their 1993 editorial essay, "Where are the Theories for the New Organizational Forms?" R. L. Daft and A. Y. Lewin forewarn us about technology's impact on the corporation when they state, "Computer-mediated communication technology is becoming the backbone of many organizations, supplanting the formal hierarchical structure to achieve coordination and manage relationships within and between organizations."[1] These writers are speaking of the impact technology had on businesses prior to the pervasive adoption of the Internet. The Web further compounds the complexities of these new organizational dynamics.

Many businesses will face an uphill battle in their attempt to alter the status quo. That's because existing organizations are stitched together like fine tapestries—every piece of thread is unique, yet each holds its place in relation to the whole. If a thread were to come loose, there is a real threat that the fabric will unravel. That's one of the reasons why executive management is so indecisive about the Web. Managers are not quite sure what to make of it—is it a thread, a tapestry, a sewing machine, or a textile factory? But they do know one thing: The Web will have an impact on their business and their organization that must be dealt with.

Business leaders aspiring to "Webify" their efforts will face tough decisions about how far they want to integrate the Web into their companies. Fundamentally, there are five key components to Webifying an organization:

- Empowering, educating, and energizing executive management to lead the Web initiative
- Transforming the hierarchical organizational structure to a system of multidirectional, interconnected alliances
- Developing employee skills sets to be Web-savvy

- Changing the way programs are funded
- Measuring performance based on new metrics

Educating and Energizing Executive Management

Perhaps the most important first step in overcoming the resistance to change brought on by the Web is for executives to take a leadership role in the process. The development and execution of a strategic Web initiative must be driven by an inspired and courageous leader with the decisive leadership skills necessary to shake up an organization's planning process from the ground up, ultimately giving birth to a new operating model for the organization. But for many companies, this type of inspired leadership isn't in place.

"The mandate for change isn't coming from the top," says InsWeb's Ticehurst. "It's coming instead from middle management. Standard business procedures don't allow middle management to coordinate initiatives with people at their level across multiple departments. Middle managers have to advance ideas up the management chain until they finally reach the executive VP level. Problem is, change doesn't happen, because you've got too many layers of management, and each has to agree before anything gets done. It's a highly inefficient process for today's competitive business environment."

A department head at a major manufacturing company summed up the Web dilemma in her company by saying, "We're a large company. The wheels turn, but sometimes they turn rather slowly. The internal mechanisms for completing a process are not always 100 percent aligned with the speed at which the Web changes. That forward-thinking mindset has not permeated upwards throughout our organization completely. We're still waiting for senior management to get on board, to drink the Web Kool-Aid, so to speak."

Companies with executive management buy-in are at an extreme advantage. This has unquestionably been key to the success of Dell, Oracle, Symantec, and many others.

"Web professionals are waiting for strategic Internet direction from the corporate executives, who are typically not fully convinced or aware of the Web as a strategic business vehicle," asserts Anthony Sanchez, Senior Manager, Internet Programs and Development, Oracle Support Services. "Big businesses have to realize that the playing field is not only leveled by the Internet, but that it's going to favor those whose entire company fully understands and embraces it."[2]

Companies like Symantec have taken the early lead, in part due to executive managers who not only "get the Web," they use it as an everyday business tool. "Symantec's CEO John W. Thompson gets the Web," claims Symantec's Roberts. "I think this gives us a competitive advantage in the market."

"We sought the endorsement from the top of the company so we could institutionalize the concept of 3M's Customer Centers," explains 3M's vice president of corporate marketing, Chuck Harstad. "By gaining endorsement at the highest levels, the message spread throughout the corporation that the Customer Center strategy is what all divisions will follow in the future. The key to our success comes from all divisions understanding the value of this strategy in growing the company."[3]

"One of the early organizational barriers that Dell had to go through was convincing everybody that the Web wasn't just a science project—that the Web could be used to conduct real business," says Dell's Langer. "I think you've got to have your CEO behind the Web effort 100 percent. And that person must articulate that vision across all management ranks of the company. Michael Dell is our strongest online advocate. It's great having him as our CEO, not only for his vision and leadership, but his commitment to the Web has been complete and total. He feels that the Web is our most strategic weapon—our strongest differentiation point."

These types of companies aren't the only ones with competitive advantage due to executive leadership. Web start-up companies that have created chaos in traditional markets such as book, music, and toy retailing are led by executives who not only "drink the Kool-Aid," but who helped make it. The advantage a Web "pure play" company (one that focuses entirely on the Web) has because its leadership is so dialed into the technology and is part of the Web "inner circle" is not to be underestimated. Lots of deals are closed during Internet conferences and other places Web insiders frequent.

"Today's Web-involved CEO understands that it takes more than a great idea and a solid business plan to prosper," says Ken Orton, formerly of Preview Travel. "Auspicious business alliances, smart strategic partnerships, and multifaceted business relationships are essential to success."

What's different about the profile of executive leaders in a Web-engaged company? CEOs of Internet-commerce companies have some common characteristics: They are experts in the operations of their unique industry, they have good heads for marketing, and they are technologically savvy. As well, they are supported by executive teams who are highly competent at executing business strategies in a Web-driven context. We will look at the typical organizational chart of these companies later in this chapter.

But if you are an existing company, without the advantage of a full Web-savvy team to help create and lead a Web strategy for your company the way Internet-commerce companies do, where do you begin? We believe that creating the right type of leadership is a critical step.

THE CHIEF WEB OFFICER

Let's take a look at a typical organization that already has a Web site and that maintains it in-house. The person who creates and maintains the site is too often a lower-level management employee many layers down in the org chart—certainly not an executive level employee. This position is a tactical job, not strategic. These employees are not plugged into the company at a business strategy level and are not empowered to make business decisions for the company. And that is perhaps the biggest mistake companies make regarding their Web strategies—they have the wrong person designated champion of the cause. This job function is relegated to performing technical and graphics support to an ancillary communications effort. But as businesses come to realize just how important the Internet is as a strategic business vehicle, the role of coordinating the Web effort must become a strategic position within the company.

The Web creates the need for an additional employee of a different level in the company—the Chief Web Officer—who is responsible for the company's Internet strategy. A new C-level position is created maybe once a decade. Before the advent of mainframe computers, for example, there was no such thing as a Chief Information Officer (CIO). This was the new C-level position in the seventies. In the eighties and nineties, it became very trendy to upgrade the level of quality of products, services, and customer service. This new, resulting C-level position was the Chief Quality Officer (CQO). Now that the Web is becoming vitally important to business across all sectors, it is reasonable to assume that the C-level job that will develop in the early 2000s will be the Chief Web Officer (CWO). The key competencies for the person serving as the CWO include an even balance of strengths in technology, business strategy, marketing, sales, customer relationship development, and customer service. And this position is the key interface to all those related organizations in the future.

This new position has a deep impact on the organizational hierarchy. When a company has a CWO making business strategy decisions for the organization, that person has a better opportunity to get things done. But she must be treated as a peer with as much organizational clout as the other decision makers in the company. Organizational politics can get pretty dicey, and a CWO who is not empowered by the organization will be dismissed by those with a different agenda. If a company is not yet ready to revamp its officer level structure, another C-level executive must be willing to step up to the plate and champion the Web cause in order for the Web strategy to be successful.

We discussed this idea at a technology conference for chief information officers who worked for all types of industries. The idea sparked a lively debate. Some agreed that the creation of such a position was warranted, given the importance of the Web to their businesses. Others were not convinced that such a position was necessary, believing instead that their position included responsibility for the Web strategy. Certainly from a technical perspective, the CIO plays a key role. But it is our experience that the CIO does not typically spend enough time with customers to understand their demands and preferences. Similarly, the CIO does not usually possess an understanding of marketing, a key component of the successful Web strategy.

Regardless of what organization spawns the position, the key point is how important the position is to a company's success on the Web. Eventually we may see the next generation of CEOs coming from this CWO position. After all, what other corporate officers will have such a comprehensive perspective on the requirements for success as an effective CWO?

As we move beyond executive management, we begin to see how the Web is impacting the entire organizational process— shaking up "silo-centric" org structures that have long dominated the traditional corporate environment. Many of today's companies are at a critical crossroads—how deep and how far should they integrate the Web into their organizations? The most successful companies will leverage the Internet as a business facilitator in order to migrate beyond individual needs, group charters, and departmental compensation schemes. Whole Experience Web sites require nothing less.

Organizational Structures

The Web is presenting some significant challenges to the typical organizational structure. Perhaps more than at any recent time, the Web creates a need for cross-organizational collaboration. Most companies are not organized for this multifunctional effort. This next section takes a look at how the need for Web expertise and involvement is impacting traditional organizations and how they need to change to accommodate the realities of competing in an online world.

Organizational Migration

When the Web first became a technical reality, many companies began adopting it as a marketing communications vehicle, the

results of which are referred to as "brochureware" sites. It is no
accident that corporate marketing departments developed these
early-generation Web sites. It was an extension of promotions
and advertising. But as the Web takes on a more primary business role that extends beyond communications, the organizational requirements must transform to accommodate Web integration
at all levels.

Cognitiative's Pulse of the Customer research confirms that
companies that historically had their Web sites managed by marketing groups are now involving other functional departments.
For instance, companies that are using their sites to deliver customer service or to conduct sales transactions are experimenting
with various combinations of collaboration, control, and maintenance, involving the IT, marketing, service, and sales departments. Figure 5.1 illustrates points at which escalating functional
complexity and strategic importance of a Web initiative require
the active involvement of varying departments, right on up to
the CEO.

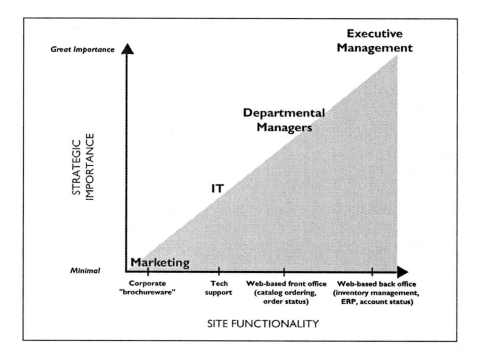

The reasons other groups need to get involved are very prag-
matic. Adding features such as password-protected access to
technical support means that the technical skills of an IT department become necessary. And as more complex functionality such
as sales transactions, inventory management, or ERP (enterprise
resource planning) are built into a site, the venture becomes
more strategic in nature—requiring deeper organizational
involvement from executive management. Highly evolved business Web sites—those that allow users to customize and negotiate complex business processes in an online business relationship, automating as many mundane business procedures as possible, require total organizational involvement.

The Trouble with Silos

Companies that have already moved their Web strategies beyond
the marketing realm are offering commerce, support, and shopping via their Web sites—many times with the right idea, but
without cohesive execution. Because these sites often evolved in
parallel inside one company without much collaboration, the sites
are often disconnected organizational "silos" for marketing, commerce, or customer support—mapped to the organization chart
responsible for that company activity. While these silo sites share
the company logo and customers, too often they don't share user
interface, navigation schemes, registration databases, and content standards. The company winds up looking fragmented; the
corporate image is diffused. But worse, the impact on the
user/customer is confusion, frustration, and potentially defection.

"Prior to the Web, we lived very well within silos," says Jim
Radford, Internet marketing services manager for 3M. "We could
create new business, new products, and new services without
bumping into customers across departments. However, when you
compress all of these activities into one common platform that
links everything together, you have a very attractive opportunity
to interconnect business functions that have common interests.
Being able to see and serve all aspects of a company simultaneously is a growth driver, and it can better serve the customer.
Before the Internet, this was not possible."[4]

"Large corporations can't coordinate information very well because there are too many layers of management that all have to agree," claims InsWeb's Ticehurst. "That's why strategic decisions have to be made at the very highest levels if you're really going to see efficiencies. Silos tend to defeat the efficiencies that the Internet offers, because the efficiencies of the Internet cross many silo boundaries. Companies have to learn how to make changes in their internal operating structure to compete in the Internet economy."

It's easy to see why this phenomenon happens—organizationally and politically. Most companies who already have a Web presence have empowered groups within the company to use the Web as a tool to solve a particular business problem that is unique to that department's or business unit's mission. Each group has its own charter, its own objectives, and its own compensation schemes tied to accomplishing certain activities or meeting certain performance goals. As a result, groups have evolved their own Web content, style, and site experience according to their business objectives and culture.

Noted Web guru, Jakob Nielsen, says that a company's Web site should not mirror its org chart. He claims that it's a trap many fall into because executive management chooses to distribute responsibility for the site to divisions and departments according to already established chains of command and budget categories. But in doing so, Nielsen asserts, a company ends up creating an "internally centered site rather than a customer-focused site."

Remember that the goal of the Whole Experience Web site is to provide a complete, fulfilling experience, no matter where the customer/user is in the Consumption Cycle. But, the purpose of each silo site does not necessarily match the objectives of what a united company site should be. When business unit Web strategies are not in concert with each other, the silos become obstacles to implementing a Whole Experience. The various groups are not given incentive to work together as one cohesive machine. Too often, executive management isn't helping, because managers don't understand the technology well enough to referee—or even to coordinate a unified solution.

So how does a company overcome this barrier? How do you structure a company so that it is not silo-centric? How do you create an environment for employees to accomplish goals and objectives that are critical to their departments, yet ensure that they also work together as a cohesive unit for the good of the organization?

Some companies try the large task force approach—where representatives from each department within a company come together as a group, contribute ideas, and try to agree on a unified solution. This method is fraught with peril because large committees often take too long to achieve results, for myriad reasons ranging from scheduling conflicts to irreconcilable political issues. And often, no *one* group or person is accountable for the outcome. The best ideas tend to happen when a small group or subgroups are given the charter to come up with a solution. For some companies that are accustomed to working in cross-functional task forces, the solution may be to improve the task force process. In any case, someone needs to step forward, take ownership of the issue, and deliver on it. A designated and respected group or leader has to ultimately be accountable and empowered to get the strategy and plan developed.

Other companies try to overcome the silo phenomenon by agreeing on a corporate look and feel—a Web style guide that functions as a veneer to mask the different silo sites from the user. This can be an effective strategy as long as companies can make the site function as if there is a cohesive infrastructure connecting all the silos together. This can be accomplished by building customized software applications that integrate one department's database with another's. If all the databases are connected together and the content can be served up to the user within a unified template, then the silo system can be made to work. There is something to be said for a company that can figure out how to make each pocket of expertise—each silo—function on that level.

Start-up companies, such as Preview Travel, eToys, and Amazon.com have an organizational advantage because they can create Whole Experience organizational structures from the beginning. If you were to peel away the outer layers of a Web-centric business, you'd find that different job titles and different departments exist within those companies as compared to traditional, established organizations.

If you're not a Web start-up company and you have to deal with existing silo org structures, the challenge for executive management is figuring out how to implement Web standards across each department that would have the same goals, strategies, messages, navigation, look and feel, design and content standards, performance metrics, and registration procedures. Executive management must take a hard look at:

- How to evolve the company vision to include the Web reality
- How to provide leadership to executive staff and line organizations
- How to compensate employees
- How to charter the group
- How to measure performance
- How to integrate departmental processes
- How to fund projects

Industrial supplies manufacturer 3M is a good example of an existing company that faced a formidable organizational task when it decided to adopt the Web as a strategic business vehicle. 3M's Chuck Harstad identified three key challenges the company faced:

- To get our people to think and act around a customer-centered philosophy, rather than to gravitate back to their product-centered silo way of thinking. That's a cultural shift that's going to take a lot of nurturing and care on the part of everybody to make it work. The fact that we've launched our Customer Centers is no guarantee they are going to work.
- Our marketing community needs to discover and understand how to leverage this channel [the Web] for growth.
- To realize that the channel opens up our greatest opportunity to capture data. How best to capture and share that data on an enterprise-wide basis, and how to then use that data to better serve our customers.

The leaders of the organization must set the guidelines and direction that will accommodate these diverse requirements in a way that moves the entire organization to the Web-strategy goal.

FUNDING

Businesses must not only examine who currently manages their corporate Web initiative, they must contemplate the best way to go from where they are to where they want to be. Inevitably, the issue of Web site funding presents a serious challenge to organizational management. Face it—funding a Whole Experience Web site is a budget line item that hasn't existed before. And for most companies, that's a real dilemma. Some companies are trying to squeeze Web site funding out of their marketing budgets. But if marketing is the only department within a company that has a Web budget, then you aren't budgeting enough to truly make the Internet a strategic business vehicle for your whole company.

The situation can be more dire if you are in a market that is being penetrated by well-funded Internet start-ups. Web start-ups have an advantage because the Web is their business—their entire budget is devoted to their Web effort. That budget can be a multimillion-dollar figure. In contrast, some established companies are having trouble committing to Web budgets in the $100,000–$500,000 range. There's a huge funding gap between those two scenarios.

Investing in the Web will have positive top-line and bottom-line returns, if the site is well executed and you are patient enough to let it succeed. Some companies have measured the investment return on their Web sites and have determined that the sites have paid for themselves many times over.

For example, as discussed in chapter 1, Cisco Connection Online (CCO) was launched in 1996 at a cost of $3 million. The bulk of the costs of were salaries. Cisco customers quickly saw the advantage of picking out prices and configuring products electronically:

- CCO provides unparalleled access to all of Cisco's critical business data
- CCO delivers the ability for customers to place orders at any time, from anywhere in the world
- CCO facilitates accurate product configuration and order entry, saving customers time and money

There are substantial benefits for Cisco as well:

- CCO saves the company money by automating the ordering process (e.g., it has shaved inaccurate orders down to less than 1 percent.)
- CCO reduces the amount of time customer service representatives spend on order processing by roughly 40 percent, freeing them up to focus on better service and relationship building
- As of early 1999, CCO processes over one thousand online orders daily, compiling $11 million in revenue per day and generating over $4 billion a year for the firm
- CCO generates 70 percent of the company's total revenues
- CCO has over 34,000 customer sites that order Cisco products exclusively online
- Over a period of three years, Cisco's value has swelled from $15 billion to more than $100 billion

All tolled, including savings harvested from manufacturing, the Internet is saving Cisco about $360 million per year and helping to preserve its greater than 32 percent operating margins.

As this example shows, the benefits and economies of scale enabled by moving business to the Web can obviously have payback to you as a vendor, both in cost reductions and increased customer satisfaction. But, as with any other business strategy, investment will be required—investment in staffing, skill development and retraining, and technology (we cover this topic in chapter 6). Analysis is needed to understand just where and how much investment should be made, weighing investment costs against projected paybacks. Then you can determine adequate funding levels to support current Web strategy as well as future growth requirements.

An interesting exercise is to assume that a new Web-commerce company is invading your market space, threatening to steal market share from you by serving your customers with a Web presence. For example, Barnes and Noble, Borders, and countless regional and locally owned bookstore chains and stores experienced this threat from Amazon. If that happened to your company, how would you respond, not only from a funding perspective, but overall?

In the bookselling arena, Barnes and Noble responded by purchasing the world's largest book distributor, Ingram Book Group, forcing Amazon.com and other booksellers to buy a significant portion of their inventory from Barnes and Noble (in fact, Ingram supplies over 50 percent of Amazon's books). Many book retailers are vigorously opposed to the deal, fearing that the new Barnes and Noble/Ingram Books company will have too much control over pricing and inventory. With multiple distribution hubs around the world, the new Barnes and Noble venture may be able to offer superior shipping times for products priced the same as Amazon.com. Barnes and Noble didn't stop with the acquisition. It sold a 50 percent share in its online store, barnesandnoble.com, to German publishing firm Bertelsmann AG before it went public in 1999—in an effort, many believe, to gain enough working capital to compete head-to-head with Amazon.

Is your company—that is, its executive leadership, organizational structure, employee skills sets, and funding models—prepared for such a competitive strike?

Organized for Success: The Web Start-Up

To work through your organizational issues, it may be useful to hypothetically design your Web organization as if you were a start-up. If you were not encumbered by the structures and politics of your current organization, how would you set up the structure most likely to succeed? To assist you in this thinking, we have assembled a prototype organizational chart based on the structures of some leading Web-commerce companies. Here we can get some insight into what types of job roles are performed and how they are organized when the Internet is your primary business vehicle.

While Internet-commerce companies have some organizational differences, there are many common elements to the departments and roles within their organizations. What's really different, however, is that all departments are now focused on the Web site. Below is a brief description of the most typical direct reports and major functional areas of these companies:

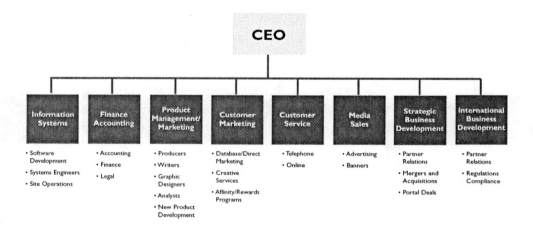

CEO (Executive Operations): Some companies have all operations reporting to the CEO. Others have chief operating officers or vice presidents of operations, who handle some operational responsibilities and report to the CEO.

Information Systems: Typically includes three major functional areas:

- Software Development (sometimes called product development): Software engineers within the company actually write the software that runs the site. These engineers are specialists in the unique type of transaction that is at the core of the business, such as interfaces to legacy reservation systems in a travel company or product-shipment tracking in a commerce company. Most Internet-commerce companies write a large portion of their own software, as the off-the-shelf software available is not fully functioned enough to serve their unique business needs.

- Systems Engineering: This group is generally responsible for designing the architecture of the system, both hardware and software.
- Site Operations: This includes the management of the data center, network, telecommunications services, systems administration, quality assurance, documentation, and training. Some companies segment out their security and fraud control, others manage those functions within site operations.

Customer Marketing: Customer acquisition is driven by this marketing department, which is typically responsible for all outbound marketing tasks such as advertising, database/direct marketing, creative services, market analysis, affinity/rewards programs, public relations, and partner relations.

Product Management/Marketing: In the Internet-commerce context, this department is tasked with customer retention and is responsible for producing the "experience." It includes people such as producers, writers, graphic designers, analysts, and new product developers. Many companies actually manage different aspects of the site experience as "products." For example, a travel site might manage leisure products separately from business products. Writers might include vacation reporters, business-news reporters, and destination reporters.

Customer Service: Despite the fact that Internet-commerce companies handle many customer service calls online, most credible companies maintain a customer service group that handles problems via telephone as well. These groups are tasked with handling both online and offline support.

Media Sales: Since most Internet-commerce sites sell advertising space and banners, there's typically a group responsible for media sales. This group is often populated by regional sales reps who work in their designated markets or industries.

Strategic Business Development: This group is responsible for creating strategic alliances with other companies on the Web. There is a significant level of alliance activity in the Web world as companies negotiate exclusive deals with portals or partner with complementary providers to extend products and services.

International Business Development: Because conducting Internet commerce outside the United States is still in developmental phases, the group responsible for international markets typically has its own department and executive leadership. Many times these groups are staffed with people who are not only expert in certain geographies but are also adept at developing strategic alliances, since many international strategies are executed through joint development with local enterprises.

Finance/Accounting: This typically includes accounting, finance, investor relations, and human resources. These functions are not especially unique in a Web environment.

Special Groups: Most Internet-commerce companies have groups that are unique to their industry and their business focus. For example, an online auction company has a group dedicated to merchandise acquisition. An online automobile buying service has a group focused on dealer and manufacturer relations.

Organized for Success: Existing Companies with Web Initiatives

Another way to work through organizational deterrents is to study the way existing companies have organized their strategic Web initiatives to coexist with time-honored business processes/practices. Currently, companies who have launched successful Web sites understand that collaboration is a key component to a prosperous Whole Experience site.

We have assembled an organizational chart based on the Web-site strategies and deployment duties that underlie some highprofile firms who have successfully integrated the Web into their businesses. This is one way, but surely not the only way, that companies are organizing for the Web. As shown in figure 5.3, the Web group often has dual reporting accountabilities, both to corporate marketing and to the IT department. While often not a direct organizational reporting structure, product marketing plays a key role in the Web presence as well.

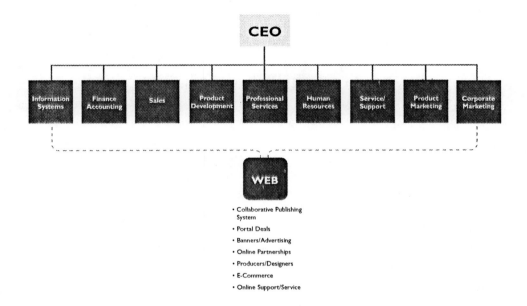

Rather than defining the roles of each part of an organization relative to the Web, we delve more deeply into the roles of corporate marketing, product marketing, and information systems, as these are the groups most dramatically changed due to the introduction of the Web.

Corporate Marketing: This group is one of the primary drivers of the corporate Web strategy. It is empowered to manage the Web site, which has evolved into a strategically important business operation. Job responsibilities involve an array of tasks that have not classically been part of a corporate marketing group, such as forging relationships with portal sites, developing and producing online content, and designing user interfaces for e-commerce transactions.

Product Marketing: This department is often the key player in the ongoing Web content–development efforts of an organization. It is the source for crucial deliverables such as product literature, white papers, FAQs, pricing, and special product promotions. One of the organizational challenges companies face is how to empower this group—and others like it in the company—to contribute content directly to the Web site rather than through an HTML bottleneck. (We talk about this more in chapter 6).

Information Systems: Most companies who have had sophisticated information systems (IS) departments have found the need to increase skills sets in several key areas so that they can rise to the technology challenges presented by the Internet. These areas include core networking infrastructure, both local area networks (LAN) and wide area networks (WAN) environments, switching, cabling, and network systems architectures. In addition, because Web sites are increasingly becoming business-critical and global, IS departments are faced with the continual battle of backing up critical data that is generated on the site. This can be especially challenging, because in the Web world, business hours are twenty-four hours a day, seven days a week. There is never a good time to bring the network down to back it up. Therefore, IS professionals must be skilled at applying advanced storage techniques to back up and archive data so as to ensure that they are prepared for a computer systems disaster.

And if those aren't enough new challenges for an already overburdened IT department, the Web is also creating the need to do more programming, in advanced technologies such as C++, object languages, and SQL databases. And new applications and technologies are rapidly being developed to address common IS requirements, such as content publishing, transaction processing, and security encryption. Keeping pace with these developments is a significant task.

Some companies are working through organizational deterrents by creating separate Web divisions within the parent company that report to a senior executive, thereby avoiding the turf wars than can erupt when companies try to manage their Web business strategy between departments. In 1996, Dell Computer did just that. Dell felt that it was necessary to set up a separate division—a center of competence within the company charged with creating the company's corporate Web experience. As Dell's

Robert Langer explains, "Rather than having Dell Online be part of our IT organization or our marketing organization, we decided to set it up to be freestanding. That way, we owned the overall strategy for Dell Online—yet we were open to input from our business partners. We factored their needs into our overall development plans."

Other companies have integrated Web-strategy initiative throughout the entire corporation, ensuring buy-in and participation from employees across all departments. Companies like 3M have adopted this strategy. As 3M's Harstad remarks, "Each of our Customer Centers is populated by a number of different divisions products. For example, in the Electronics Manufacturing Customer Center, eight major stakeholder divisions and seven minor stakeholder divisions participate. That is a real change from the past, where a single division thought about their specific products and customers. Now, with the Web, all fifteen of our divisions have to work in a collaborative environment. The result, hopefully, is a site that is easy for our customers to understand—leveraging all of 3M's products to a single customer base."

Most companies have evolved through several organizational approaches. While each approach may have caused some internal angst, every step of the process has provided critical knowledge about how to be a more Web-effective organization. Truly an evolution, a sequence of organizational transformations is required to come to the most successful state of being—and it will never be static.

Developing Employee Skills Sets to be Web-Savvy

The Internet boom has had a ripple effect on businesses in all sectors, prompting many firms to take a closer look at the new skills sets required of its employees. It stands to reason that if the Web has become such a dramatic force in business, it will have a significant impact on required personnel skills. Back in 1996, for example, Dell Computer was able to develop and launch Dell Online with only twelve employees, mostly engineering talent who had basic HTML development skills. A successful company like Dell would not be able to launch a similar Web site in today's market. The bar has been raised too high.

This affects not only hiring practices, but also training curriculum for on-the-job skill set development. iOwn.com's Ned Hoyt explains, "The Web changes almost every aspect of the business . . . so we have to bring in people who have traditional skills sets and also a willingness to learn the way things happen in a Web environment."

These new skills are not limited to duties such as programming, Web design, and information management. We're talking about thinking and working completely with an Internet mindset, and we're talking about knowing how it works and knowing what is possible.

In reality, job profiles change the moment a company commits to a Web business strategy. As can be seen in the organizational structures in the previous section, the Web creates the need for newly defined job roles and, as well, places new demands on employees in more traditional positions.

Cisco's Chris Sinton affirms that assessment when he says, "We have an entire interactive marketing tools group working within the organization. Where were those positions four years ago? They didn't exist."

Not only does this create jobs, it also creates new demands on employees already working in an organization. Even if existing employees have the talent and ability to pick up new skills sets, they don't necessarily have the time in their busy schedules to take on the extra workload. The downsizing trend that happened from the 1980s to the 1990s left most companies fairly lean. To add more responsibility to an already full plate is a problem. Executive management has to determine what is possible for employees to accomplish in an eight- to ten-hour day so that "a day's work" becomes a task employees can handle. Contributing content to a Web site is not something an employee should try to squeeze in after 6:00 P.M.

In addition, employees on the front lines of any business—the salesperson, the customer service representative, the purchasing agent—must be informed, educated, and empowered in order to perform their jobs well. Armed with critical need-to-know information, the required tools, and the ability to act, workers can become more productive and valuable to the enterprise.

Our Pulse of the Customer research consistently reveals that employees are often not given the tools necessary to perform their jobs online, even though they want to be more Web-involved. For example, many procurement specialists identify the root cause of not using the Web more extensively for corporate procurement as an inability to both technically integrate procurement policies into Web-based purchasing systems and, as well, to interface Web transactions with legacy accounting systems. Even when Web purchasing is an option, existing EDI systems or ordering via telephone is often easier.

Some of the skills sets are scarce, and there's a limited supply of qualified talent from which to draw. For these types of jobs, such as software developers, site producers, and site operations professionals, employers are relegated to drawing talent from a small group of qualified technology candidates who are very particular about the type of company they want to work for. Larger, more established companies who need talented people to run their Internet operations have an especially difficult challenge, because they have to compete with new Internet-commerce companies for new hires. What's more appealing to a prospective employee—working for an established company and helping it to migrate its business operations to the Web, or working for a start-up company, investing in its stocks, and driving it toward an IPO?

Regardless of how a company recruits for or assigns Web responsibilities, the reality is that new skills sets are required all around—from the manager to the individual contributor in the field. A collective effort will be needed to help make the transition.

Executive Management

As the Web moves from a secondary marketing function to a primary business vehicle, the skills, competencies, and knowledge expected from today's business leaders are changing. The Whole Experience requires the leadership skills of an authoritative representative who understands the company's entire business strategy—its marketing, sales, fulfillment, support, IT, financial, and Web strategies.

In order to be prepared to make wise decisions in new and complex areas, executives must possess an array of skills sets that are crucial for survival in today's competitive environment. The most prominent of these skills sets include:

- Comprehending the business impact of the Web—the trade-offs, risks, and potential
- Understanding technical possibilities and the ability to discuss complex subjects with subordinates
- Possessing strong communication skills and the ability to articulate what the Internet strategy should be
- Understanding the competitive landscape and the needs of business partners, and how the Internet factors into these relationships
- Having enthusiasm for the Web and a willingness to take risks
- Having Web experience—as a businessperson and as a consumer

Executive management must be prepared to make tough decisions—and stand by those decisions. Of course, executives are accustomed to making tough decisions, but the Web often presents management with decisions that are new and with which they don't have much experience. For example, one decision that is particularly difficult is deciding how and where to invest in the required technical infrastructure. There are many unknowns in the decision. First, you don't know what the overall site traffic ultimately will be, so determining how much capacity to buy is a crapshoot. Second, many of the software solutions are so new and untested that for most people, choosing one over another requires a lot of study and a leap of faith. We have seen large companies face similar decisions about which Web application software they should choose. Amazingly, their decisions on what solutions to adopt were very different, even though their needs and specifications were exactly the same. That's an indication of how immature the Web application software market really is—and that's a very scary state to be in when a manager is trying to make a decision about which application to build its Web strategy on.

Another difficult decision an executive must make in relation to Web initiative is whether to develop the site in-house or outsource it. It is common for companies to outsource the development and maintenance of their Web sites, because they recognize that the competencies required are beyond what they have on staff in their IT departments. It's a classic "make versus buy" decision. While it is of strategic importance to have a killer Web site, it is not strategically necessary to have the competencies in-house to do it—at least, at this time. This was a common approach in the 1960s with the initial commercial availability of mainframes. Companies outsourced the management of their data centers to other firms, such as Electronic Data Systems, because they didn't have the resources in-house to perform these tasks at this early stage in the adoption of computer technology. Later, as more people became skilled at computer operations, more companies began building their own information systems departments. In the Web context, outsourcing will be popular in the short term but will eventually be brought back in-house once people are more comfortable with their technology skills.

The CEO of the future will likely be a skilled "road warrior" who knows how to use technology to optimize his job performance and time management.

THE MARKETING PROFESSIONAL

In traditional marketing, there are professionals who specialize in standard marketing processes using time-honored vehicles for achieving the desired results. These are people who specialize in advertising, PR campaigns, collateral material, direct marketing, market analysis, and trade shows. When the Web becomes the primary vehicle for communicating with markets, these traditional skills sets become incomplete and potentially even obsolete. The key is to figure out how to utilize the employees you already have within your marketing department so that they become productive in a Web-marketing context. Executive management must take stock of existing personnel and the competencies that they possess and help them to become Web-savvy.

In light of the barriers, the direct marketing position is a great example of one that needs to be redefined. That is, the professional in this position needs to get smart to how the Web can empower her to achieve her marketing agenda. The Internet is definitely the direct marketing channel of the next century. Today's marketing person has to know how to contribute to and extract information from the Web. How else can a marketing person use data from a company's user registration system to perform marketing tactics such as mass customization or one-to-one marketing? If the direct marketing professional is ignorant of the capabilities of the database technology, or if she is not empowered to interact with the company's content publishing system, then she will never be able to take full advantage of all that an integrated system has to offer.

That's not to say that marketing professionals need to be programmers but, rather, that they should be able to have a meaningful interchange with the development team and understand what it is doing with the Web site. What we've observed is that there is a lack of communication and understanding—a lack of a common terminology between marketing and technology professionals. This creates a barrier in developing effective Web strategies. Marketers don't know what's technically feasible, and Internet technology personnel don't understand the marketing methodologies of the organization.

A new profession or skills set is evolving in the marketing group—a combination marketing and functionality strategist. The new position requires an employee skilled in both areas and, as well, a keen understanding of technology at a conceptual/functional level and also an understanding of marketing strategy at a high level. Marketing departments can't trust that the IT department will make the right Web marketing decisions for them. That means that the marketing professional has to understand technology topics, such as personalization and when to use it, profiling and how marketing can elevate profile information, registration techniques and how to motivate people to register on the site, and dynamic content generation and its implications on content development.

Another example of how marketing skills sets are changing is to look at the role of the advertising specialist. Today's ad experts have to know about new issues that go beyond what they may have learned in college. Several issues—for example, how the Web empowers customers, how people like to communicate online, what ad techniques work online, who the major players are in the Web space, how people search the Web to find information they need, the limitations of technology, and how a company gets noticed online—are all topics about which today's advertising specialists must be savvy. It's almost as if the traditional knowledge base about what ad experts know about the customer and the medium has been turned on its ear. Traditional advertising specialists—and marketing professionals in general—have a lot of new issues and information to digest.

So how will this change come about? Many marketing experts will have to be retrained to be able to take on the Web. It's impractical to think that every existing employee will become obsolete because of the Web. Many traditional marketing and advertising programs and Web programs will coexist for some time. But the vice president of marketing in today's market should be looking at every opportunity for her employees and herself to learn new skills sets and to experiment with new ideas. Marketing executives should take a skills set inventory by specialty and figure how to close the gap between what their staff knows and what they need to know when the Web is the major marketing vehicle within the company.

There are many ways of approaching the issue. Some employees could be retrained by partnering with a consulting agency that knows how to do business in this space. There are some innovative education programs that are available through organizations like the American Marketing Association and the Direct Marketing Association. Moreover, there is a lot to learn by studying the Web practices of people working in other companies in their industry. How do they do things? Which of their best practices can be implemented in the department? Whichever approach is chosen, organizations should sponsor and encourage Web skills development as the next logical step in preserving the investment they've made in employees who are valuable to the effort on many other levels.

THE INFORMATION TECHNOLOGY (IT) PROFESSIONAL

Employees in the IT department have as much to learn about how to use Web technology as the employees in marketing department. But instead of only learning about the core technologies, IT professionals must also learn how those technologies impact a company's business processes and customer relationships.

The IT employees have to understand who the players are within the organization, how each department works together, who to believe, and who to listen to. Plus, they need to understand the full specifications of what's required from business strategy and customer requirements standpoints. Developing customer empathy is critical. Too many times we've heard IT professionals say that the customer will "just have to figure it out," rather than taking a "how can I make this easier for the customer" attitude.

In addition, the technology decisions are increasingly complex. There are new layers of decisions that have to be made, such as deciding on what types of systems should be used for content development, publishing, and management. Some IT professionals are making decisions based on a company's existing staffing paradigm—assuming there is always going to be an HTML expert on staff who functions as the Webmaster—a person who has the ability to mark up content and post it to the Web. If you assume that the world is not going to change and you make an IT platform decision based on that assumption, then you are relegating the company to commit to a technology that may soon become obsolete. Such poor decisions can create huge problems. To avoid such costly blunders, today's IT professional must be in sync with management in all departments and continually evolve with technology trends.

In addition, the more dependent a company is on its Web site, the more critical it is that the IT manager has a business continuance plan—that is, knowledge of what the procedure will be if the system goes down, what are the backup and recovery practices? Resolving disaster-related issues is increasingly complex in a networked world, and potential disasters must be anticipated.

THE WRITER/EDITOR

Writing effective material for the Web is decidedly different from drafting a business report or churning out advertising copy. It requires a unique set of skills to successfully translate business jargon, sophisticated marketing terminology, and subliminal sales pitches into compelling, high-impact Web copy.

Based on our research in this area, prospects, customers, employees, and shareholders want Web sites to engage them and help them become more productive. This means that businesses can't simply regurgitate sales and promotional material onto the computer screen. A Web site's unique organizational structure, hyperlinks, and intense competition for user attention requires Web writers to present their written content in a way that best suits the unique needs of the site's target audience.

Of course, it's possible for online writers to reuse company brochures, direct mail pieces, product catalogs, press releases, newsletters, sales guides, financial reports, and other written material on the Web. But just because you can reuse content, it doesn't always mean you should. Most content, especially text, was never intended to be showcased on a computer screen. It was specifically written and designed by traditional writers for offline mediums such as print magazines and brochures.

The challenge is that writing for the Web is different. Writing for the Web can be described as an amalgam of math, story-telling, and design—held in place by intelligent hypermedia, the foundation of interactivity. Interactivity adds to the writing equation the power of participation, the ability to have a customer, vendor, or IS manager interact with the material being presented onscreen. That means that writing for an online environment requires a deep understanding of how interactive experiences can engage more than one sense to stimulate the user's interest. The trick is how to best supply this written material within a stimulating graphic and spatial environment while allowing the user to determine the pace, or "path," of information consumption.

Web writers must create copy that is alive—didactic and gripping text that cedes a portion of the author's control to the audience, allowing users to purchase products, seek out help, or self-educate. Web sites invite a user's interaction in ways distinguished both in scale and in kind from older technologies. Great sites—dynamic sites—push the boundaries of a user's imagination. Since Web users don't read every word presented on the screen, onscreen text needs to be to the point, compelling, and tightly structured. Its tone should speak the language of users and engage them in a way that services their information or transaction needs.

Many of today's top Internet-commerce companies have gone so far as to hire staff writers to craft original news stories, feature articles, business reports, case studies, online reviews, and other original content for their Web sites, resulting in much richer and targeted sites for their visitors and customers. These companies recognize the Web's strategic imperative to their business, and they've hired Web content experts to help them write and present the best possible content.

Creating original and engaging online material is a process that needs to start early in the site production cycle. Many companies are integrating marketing and mixed-media campaigns into one integrated cross-media solution—with the Web site as the primary distribution and archive center for a company's outbound messages. A Web site's collaborative publishing environment allows writers to contribute original content into pre-designed templates, with preapproved design standards, so they can concentrate on creating timely, interactive copy that reaches out to the online user.

To be successful in the Web space, writers need to get up to speed on the latest tools and techniques that enable them to create this type of rich, rewarding content. In a sense, they need to start thinking like designers and programmers in order to gain the necessary skills, insight, and respect needed to effectively create for the electronic mediums.

CREATIVE SERVICE SPECIALISTS/GRAPHIC DESIGN PROFESSIONALS

In the Web world, creativity is more important than ever. Web users crave experiences that are passionate, sophisticated, informative, useful, and easy to use—intelligence married to a digital canvas. At first glance, creative service professionals (graphic design experts) appear to be doing what they've always done—building beauty and order out of content chaos. But the advent of the Web has increased the required design skills sets of creative service specialists to a newer, higher dimension. As well, it is all too often that the graphic designer has not been trained to think about all the activities that online constituents need to do in one logical continuum on a Web site—resulting in Web experiences that fall short of their intended goals.

The embodiment of the Whole Experience is a Web site designed for the screen with a sense of balance—a fusion of layout, design, navigation, and messaging. Today's businesses face the exciting challenge of transforming their Web sites into dynamic user experiences that are more productive and engaging for people at all points of the Consumption Cycle. Graphic design specialists must craft online environments that strike a balance between process and content, between information and analysis, and between group and individual efforts. With this knowledge, companies should strive to hire creative service specialists skilled in both traditional graphic design and online design.

THE CUSTOMER SUPPORT PROFESSIONAL

Traditional customer service employees are good verbal communicators. They specialize in solving customer problems via the telephone, are adept at answering difficult questions or handling hostile confrontation, and serve as ambassadors of the parent company's brand. But the method through which these tasks are performed is changing as the Web becomes the new vehicle for customer/company communication.

Skills such as problem solving and communication are still important, but Web customer support personnel need to add additional skills to their repertoire. For example, writing and grammar are skills that traditional customer service representatives never had to consider. Support has primarily been conducted verbally via the phone, with the customer representative jotting notes on a pad of paper. The notes were for the rep's eyes only—they were not to be consumed or read by the customer. But when the Web is the preferred communication vehicle, written replies are sent to customers via e-mail. Not only do customers expect the reply to their query to be written using complete sentences and good grammar, they expect the reply to solve their problem. Customer support representatives who do not possess strong written communication skills will have a difficult time adjusting to this new way of supporting the customer.

Some companies are addressing the written communications issue by creating standard reply templates and databases that can help customer service reps quickly put together comprehensible answers to commonly asked questions. Some even go so far as to provide their reps with e-mail response forms that reps fill out for each particular customer's problem. The forms are named and are available in an internal database for reps to select and use as needed.

"In customer service, for example, you have a different kind of person working for you now than you had in the past," asserts Symantec's Roberts. "You need someone who is used to doing business online or supporting customers who do business online. It's an Internet skills set, the understanding of what the Internet is, how it works, how to navigate it, and all of that. Previously, someone had a headset and a phone. Now, your customer service people need to have some shared knowledge about using the Internet as part of the solution."

For the short term at least, customer support departments need well-rounded employees skilled in both traditional and technology-aided solutions.

THE SALES AND DISTRIBUTION PROFESSIONAL

As more and more companies experiment with the Internet, encouraging customers and prospects to buy direct from a company's Web site, many employees who function as sales and distribution intermediaries for companies are getting a bit edgy. Their fears are well founded. More and more businesses are turning to the Internet to cut costs, increase profits, and improve customer satisfaction. Many employees who function as sales intermediaries believe that the corporate desire to fuel the Web Consumption Cycle is pushing them out of the picture—and may eventually displace them.

How are traditional job functions in sales changing? Let's examine a hypothetical insurance company that decides to invest in a Web strategy that enables its sales agents to interface with new and prospective clients via the Web. The new system has the ability to completely transform the job requirements of every sales agent—from the classic salesperson to a high-profile account manager.

The traditional, "nonconnected" insurance agent spends a portion of his time servicing existing clients and his remaining time looking for new prospects. A company connected to the Web, however, can do things differently. It can utilize the Internet to market insurance services, qualify sales leads, and even sell policies online. Rather than having its sales agents spend valuable time chasing down sales leads, a Web-involved insurance company can offer its customers a higher caliber of customer service than its offline competitors—similar to the personal service provided by a financial broker.

As a lead generator for the agents, the Web can be designed to distribute sales leads to individual agents by geographic region. But these leads are not like normal leads that require an agent to close a deal by "selling" a service. Web-generated leads are really prequalified prospects who are waiting for an agent to call them and confirm the insurance coverage requested online. Instead of traditionally servicing, say, seventy-five clients and wasting a lot of time chasing down leads, the Web-empowered sales agent manages a portfolio of five hundred clients and spends her time building relationships and better servicing her clients.

This example demonstrates how the Web has the potential to alter the role and job functions of entire intermediary positions—especially in the area of sales and distribution. Rather than resisting technical changes that appear to threaten the status quo, companies should instead examine how new technologies might transform job functions to the benefit of all involved parties. In such a scenario, it is easy to foresee a day when a company not only saves money by embracing the Web, but in which the classic salesperson will evolve into a new type of employee—a corporate representative skilled in customer service, financial planning, and account solutions.

MEASURING PERFORMANCE

It is interesting to examine the MBOs (management by objectives) of employees and to do a gap analysis of what their job descriptions dictate versus what tasks they are expected to perform. Many companies have not closed the gap on job performance expectations when it comes to employees' roles vis-à-vis the Web. Why is that? Partly because it has happened so quickly and partly because it is unclear what should be measured.

The key to knowing how to measure an employee's Web-related performance is to know how to measure the performance of the actual Web site. Do you expect more sales leads, shorter sales cycles, increased sales transactions, perpetually up-to-date content, decreased customer support calls, increased customer satisfaction, etc.? All of these performance improvements are possible with the right Web strategy.

Just as it would in any business situation, employees' job descriptions must reflect what is expected of them, and metrics must be assigned to determine their level of success. The Web scenario is no different. But unfortunately, in this rapidly changing area of business, many companies have not accurately grasped what is really required to be successful on the Web, and they have not aligned job descriptions and MBOs with their Web strategy.

Properly executing this alignment is important, not just to ensure overall Web success, but also to attract and keep quality Web-related employees. Since the Web is so young, the talent pool is too small to staff all the new jobs that are emerging. Compensation is highly competitive for the best talent. Enabling and measuring the success of these employees is key to their job satisfaction and the length of time they work for your organization.

Conclusion

Stuart Wolff, president of Realtor.com, says that in the online world, the rate of change today is unprecedented, and the need for companies to think "outside of the box" is a business imperative.

As long as funding problems plague an organization and departmental barriers persist, as long as employees in competing silos are compensated according to different criteria, and as long as creating a cohesive Web site is not a primary goal of all employees, the Whole Experience Web site may be impossible to pull off.

Today's businesses face the unenviable challenge of creating flexible organizational structures and funding models that will work in the increasingly Web-connected corporate environment. Successful organizations will be driven by executive leaders who understand the strategic importance the Web presents, and who will be emboldened—rather than frightened—by the successes and failures of those who've ventured into the online space before them.

Chapter Six

Invest in the Necessary Technology to Make the Effort Successful

"The e-business model is forcing companies to redefine their core competency—to make key decisions about technology that will impact their entire operations."

—Ken Orton, former President and CEO, Preview Travel

While the thrust of this book is the strategic use of the Web as a business vehicle, no discussion of managing that strategy is complete without some understanding of the technical side of this rather technical medium. The underlying structure of Web sites is increasingly complex and sophisticated, being driven by the advancing demands and expectations of online customers. Products and technologies change on what seems like a daily basis. Even nontechnical executives and business strategists need a basic comprehension of the technical capabilities and infrastructure required to deliver a successful Web encounter to the customer.

In this chapter, we'll present an overview of the key functionalities required for a Whole Experience site, so that you, as a business strategist, can have a context in which to make the necessary investment decisions to support your Web strategy.

As a prelude to this discussion, we trust that the reader is familiar with the basics of the networked world that have evolved in the last decade, such as the proliferation of personal computers, the role of local and wide-area networks, and the world of desktop-related technologies, which have come to be a part of standard business systems in the 1990s. With that understanding, we'll explore several areas of recent technology development, the understanding of which is essential to creating sites that will deliver anything beyond static content (i.e., "brochureware") to the user.

A 1998 report, "The Emerging Digital Economy," published by the United States Department of Commerce, Economics, and Statistics Administration, projects that, by 2002, the Internet may be used for over $300 billion worth of commerce between businesses, with consumer commerce going even beyond that.[1] It also projects as many as one billion people being connected to the Internet by 2005. That represents a staggering market opportunity and an amazingly fast evolution of a new business paradigm. It also means that getting online isn't just a competitive advantage; it's quickly becoming a matter of survival.

The thrust of this expansion is increased customer convenience and satisfaction, productivity improvements, and cost. reductions. This expansion is also driving a huge increase in technology investments. Web product and service companies are cropping up everywhere. But choosing and successfully implementing the right technologies can be complex and time consuming.

For instance, Victoria's Secret (*www.victoriassecret.com*), popular women's lingerie and clothing retailer, reportedly took almost three years from initial planning to get "live" online, citing design challenges, integration with existing catalog systems, and market timing issues as greatly impacting site development and launch.[2]

In late 1998, International Data Corporation, a leading analyst for the information technology industry, hosted an Internet Executive Forum, in which participants concluded that the top constraints for getting revenue supporting applications online are the skills gap between the Web team and traditional IS and the technical integration of Web systems with core business systems. The solutions to these challenges can take a variety of forms, such as investing in new technologies, replacing core business systems, and outsourcing the labor and even the systems themselves—all possible strategies that must be evaluated in as thorough a manner as any other major strategic business decision.

Making sound investment choices requires that you understand the technical and business parameters within which the choices will be made. To design, install, support, and maintain a successful Whole Experience Web site is a substantial commitment that involves a planned and focused investment of resources. While up-front costs may seem high, not properly preparing your site to meet market expectations is more costly in the long run.

One of the exciting yet frustrating things about the Internet is that traffic to your Web site can increase dramatically at any given time. When a visitor first comes to your site, you've got one shot to make a positive first impression—that includes response time, ease of navigation, visual appeal, and satisfactory performance of the core business functions that bring people to your site in the first place. Achieve this, and you will have satisfied return customers. But miss the mark, and your brand, your site, and its mission are diminished—the online world offers too many other choices, and your competitors are just a click away.

Ensuring a positive experience is a direct result of the technology investment you make in designing the site and preparing for the unpredictable traffic volume that is the nature of online business. In the Victoria's Secret situation, they had to prepare for major surges in traffic—anticipating as many as one thousand visitors per second at peak times. Limited, Inc./Victoria's Secret CIO Jon Ricker says, "If you come out with a half-baked site, a lot of folks won't come back."[3]

Ken Orton explains his experience with IT investment: "We felt we needed three times more capacity than our average run rate needs, but we know that the first experience of a busy signal is damaging to the brand. While initial costs may have been higher than expected, growth has been higher than expected as well, because consumers are moving to e-commerce sites at a very rapid pace."

This belief is confirmed by other e-commerce executives. "We've all underestimated costs and effort required to be an Internet-commerce business," explained Levitan of E-greetings Network. "For example, in the IT area, our commitment goes higher than expected in terms of infrastructure and the people to build it." It's important to analyze not only what your site requirements may be today, but to build in the ability to handle the additional capacity that will be required as your business grows.

Enabling the Consumption Cycle

Throughout this book, we've been discussing how the Whole Experience Web site needs to support the entire Consumption Cycle—shopping, buying, delivering, and supporting—to satisfy customers' expectations of their Web experience. At the heart of this process is the ability of the customer to effect successful online transactions at each phase of the cycle.

For example, the customer must be able to determine if a desired product is available, find out what it costs, order it, potentially change the order, pay for it (or establish a means by which payment will be made, such as supplying a purchase order number), check on the order's status, and obtain shipping information. Each of these steps involves a transaction—an online activity or system request—which updates one or more master files and provides a history and audit trail.

Servers Drive the Process

Transactions are managed through servers. A server is a computer resource (which can be software or hardware or both) that is shared by multiple users (referred to as clients), which is the engine where the "back-end" processing of requests is done. It is useful to think of the Internet as an enormous multitiered client/server system. Requests are submitted by a user through a

Web browser on a client computer and passed through a series of servers, each with a specific function or set of functions, until the requested data is identified and passed back up the network to the client.

The transactions in the Consumption Cycle are managed by different types of servers that are responsible for different phases of request processing. The number of transactions that must be processed is key to determining how many servers will be required to provide satisfactory system performance in answering submitted requests. This is where the result of the investment decision is critical. Inadequate investment will produce a transaction bottleneck that slows down response times and delivers an unsatisfactory customer experience.

Looking again to Victoria's Secret, the company needed to ensure that paying customers enjoyed satisfactory system performance and were not slowed down by the mass volumes of e-voyeurs who were expected to come to the site for "aesthetic" purposes only. So, they engineered the site's servers in order to prioritize the transactions and requests from those shoppers actually making purchases. If systems handling purchase transactions get overburdened by visitors who are "just looking," servers designated for nonrevenue tasks (such as video clips of runway models) will automatically convert over to support the purchasing transactions.[4]

The end results were mixed. The site drew upwards of 1.5 million visitors on February 3, 1999. As a cross-media event tied to the biggest sporting extravaganza in the world, the Victoria's Secret Super Bowl advertisement—a made-for-the-Internet fashion-show video Webcast—generated enormous audience pull. However, extremely high site traffic left many fashion-show patrons to witness a choppy, out-of-sync video feed. Moreover, due to technical glitches, a number of America Online subscribers could not tap into the online fashion show at all.

The formula for devising the required number of different types of servers is not an exact science. There are multiple issues to be considered. First there is the hardware—the physical machines with sufficient processing power to process the volume of transactions. Regarding Preview Travel, for example, Ken Orton says, "We initially underestimated how many servers we thought we would need. But we built our infrastructure to be open and scaleable, so it's a no-brainer to add more capacity by adding more servers."

There is also the software side of the server model, dedicated to managing specific functions in the transaction flow. It is possible for multiple software servers to reside on a hardware server. Figuring out how to configure these systems is a job for the technical folks.

Software such as Web servers (the interface between the browser and the site being accessed) and application servers (the "middleware" that manages the interface with the databases where requested data is resident) are integral to the Web-commerce process. The complete systems that make up and feed into your site can physically reside in different places, depending on your needs and budget. For example, you may have some in-house system components along with other core components shared with an Internet service provider (ISP) who outsources management of your site. Or, your business may be at a stage where you want to host and manage your entire site in-house. Whether you decide to "make or buy" the architecture, servers will be an integral part of the functioning of the many processes involved with a site.

These combined technologies must work together as seamlessly as possible because they directly drive a user's experience with your site. There is a proliferation of companies developing these kinds of products. Be sure to carefully evaluate and test components under consideration for integration and compatibility during the selection process. And once you have established a fundamental architecture that works, stick with it. You will have invested in core functional systems and have built staff expertise in their use. Keep the number of new, untested products to a minimum, and you will greatly decrease the likelihood of difficulties.

ONLINE SECURITY

The processing of online transactions brings up another strategic issue—security. In the early era of commercial Web use, the Internet was widely perceived (and rightly so) to be an insecure medium. Stories of hackers and online thieves made international headlines and created an inherent fear in the minds of millions of potential online shoppers that the Web was not a safe place to supply personal data. This is, in fact, one of the primary factors that held e-commerce back from an even earlier explosion.

As Web computing has become more complex, with a growing number of servers and data transfer points, transaction security is more vital than ever. Because of the success of companies like Amazon.com, customers now know that online security can be achieved. Your customers must have that level of comfort in doing online business with you. Word travels fast on the Internet—one leak, one stolen or misused credit card number, and your site will quickly have a reputation as an insecure place of business. That may seem unfair, in that other nonWeb businesses occasionally have these problems as well. But, as with most new or unfamiliar things, a medium that is still in its infancy can provoke over-cautious behavior.

The advent of new encryption technologies, such as Secure Socket Layers (SSL) and Transaction Layer Security (TLS), have made secure transactions possible. Known as protocols, they are combined with other authentication technologies (electronic stamps or flags on data that verify its origin and legitimacy) to provide safe data transmission. These days, supplying your credit card online can be as safe or safer than giving it over a cell phone or handing it to a waiter who disappears with it before bringing your charge slip to your table.

Many leading companies are posting security policies on their Web sites to carefully explain their commitment and give the customer an extra level of comfort. These policies cover issues such as the use of credit card numbers and other personal information. America Online, for example, posts a privacy policy regarding what data it gathers about its site visitors and what it does and doesn't do with this data. AOL pays special attention to protecting the privacy and safety of children who use its services. The Preview Travel security policy assures its customers about credit card encryption and financial protection. You may want to consider posting such a policy on your site if your e-business will present any particular concerns for online customers.

THE COMMON DATABASE

The other very important type of technology in the Consumption Cycle foundation is the common database. In most companies, "islands" of data have propagated throughout the enterprise, which are captured and stored in ways that serve the unique requirements of specific functional areas. Sometimes they communicate easily with other functional departments, sometimes they don't. As organizations continue to capture more and more data, the number of databases and database users grows, compounding system complexity and the workload of the IT staff who maintain and support them. This can mean increased staff costs (more employees, more overtime, more contractors) and potentially frustrated, unproductive employees who can't get the information they need when they need it.

In the Web world, the sharing of information and ease of data access is critical to the customer experience and your competitiveness. Customers have traditionally obtained information from companies they do business with via the telephone or through courier services. The Web is changing that. People are turning to the Web site as a primary interface with a corporation throughout the Consumption Cycle. That means information usually received through other channels must now be made available via the Web site—and when the customer wants it.

According to Aaron Downey, president and CEO of round-peg, a leading edge, San Francisco–based Web-development company, "Common databases provide content to users outside the corporate environment in a better, more personalized fashion. Users can now get the data they need for themselves."[5]

Common databases help to enable a positive Web experience by simplifying the user's encounter. The common database lets the system "recognize" a customer by collecting all data relevant to that customer and associating it with a password issued upon the user's initial registration on the site. This information can then be easily retrieved during subsequent visits by triggering hidden "cookies," which allow content to be presented in a personalized form to the visitor. This helps streamline the processing of queries, speed up response times, and provide around-the-clock access to information. Common databases also benefit the IT staff within the company, which now has less complex systems to maintain.

Please note that when we say common database, we do not advocate a return to the cumbersome, centralized mainframe computing model. The paradigm has shifted to mixed platforms, including the server model we've already discussed. What is important is maintaining as many licensed copies of the same database as are required for your business parameters and making them centrally located and accessible to customers and employees who need them. This may involve maintaining exact copies of the database and server files in other physical locations in order to accommodate the accessibility needs of customers and staff in remote locations. For instance, site users in London will be on a very different time schedule with different business demands, peak traffic periods, and support availability needs than users in California. When systems must be available on a "follow-the-sun" basis, it's useful to have replicated content in different locations. This is accomplished through the process of "mirroring."

In mirroring, an exact copy of all files on a server is maintained at a remote site or sites and is updated and synchronized simultaneously with any changes made to the files on the master system. All users have access to the same data regardless of their location. This increases the likelihood of a positive site experience for your customers and can improve productivity of employees who do not work in-house, who may rely on Web access to get data critical to their jobs. The practice of mirroring is also helpful as a disaster protection measure—should a disaster strike one physical location where data is stored, you will have another copy in a safe, alternate location.

Mirroring does involve an extra investment, in that all systems are duplicated in one or possibly several other locations. You must invest in data lines that can accomplish long-distance data transfer at extremely high speed. Also, encryption technology is required to accomplish secure transfer of data over the Internet between mirrored systems. All this additional investment should be evaluated in terms of the payback in satisfactory user experiences, the geographic scope of your business, and your data security requirements.

If a common database is integral to your company's successful Whole Experience, then defining the common database architecture becomes a strategic decision. There are multiple options of types of database technology you can use. Throughout the 1980s and 1990s, relational database management systems (RDBMS) became a very popular way to manage data that previously had been stored in slow, cumbersome, flat-file systems. Large corporations such as Oracle and Sybase were founded on publishing RDBMS products, which have been very well received in the corporate, academic, and government computing environments over the last fifteen years. This type of technology is a safe bet and an excellent foundation for processing large volumes of data.

However, while relational databases can continue to serve organizations well, another type of database—the object database—is well worth considering for Web environments. With object databases, data can be captured as objects—collections of related information stored together. Take, for example, the idea of user-related data in the computing environment. A user record may have multiple pieces of information associated with it, such as company and address data, contact history, and purchase orders placed. In an object database model, all data about that user is stored together as an object. This eliminates the need to relate various data fields in the relational database model. The result is a faster response time to submitted queries. The object model also requires a reduced amount of coding and is particularly well suited for handling large multimedia files, such as sound and video, which you may want to incorporate into your Web site for a leading-edge look and feel.

Of course, the common database solution is not without its challenges. Unless you are starting a brand new company, you undoubtedly already have significant amounts of data captured in your organization. You will have to choose a solution that either converts your existing database applications to the new common database format or transparently and quickly communicates with other existing data repositories throughout the company.

This implementation will not be easy. Those in the technical areas of an organization tend to develop strong feelings about the technology they use. Getting them to switch can be a challenge. Also, transferring existing applications from one database to another can be time consuming, costly, and often technically challenging. Compatibility issues and varying version levels of software can increase the technical complexity. Staff already inundated with heavy workloads may not have time to add on the additional task of providing data to the new, common system. There are also the psychological issues involved with releasing the "ownership" of data and the career security and control sensitivities that may accompany such a shift.

Roundpeg's Aaron Downey relayed an experience with one of his clients, a worldwide credit card company: "This company is internationally known. They have databases around the world with tons of data. It's extremely hard to pull that data together. We had to fight with a particular department for data needed for an application to run against the common database we're building. But that department was refusing to give it up because that meant they would have to take staff people off other projects to do this. They just didn't have the time—and they really didn't want to make the information available."

This situation is not unique. Just because technology is changing very quickly does not mean that all organizations can move at the same pace. Management must understand both the business *and* technical frameworks that are required for the organization to move forward. Then, it must demonstrate leadership and confidence in how the organization should adapt to comply with the new rules.

Target Your Site to Your Visitor's Desired Experience

Another strategic use of the common database, and probably the highest priority for Whole Experience Web sites, is capturing and using data about your site visitors. The Web is changing the traditional models of marketing and customer service—the customer is now much more in control. Hence, providing the kind of experience they want is key. You and your organization must be conditioned to think and respond in terms of the full customer experience and design your site from that perspective.

With Victoria's Secret, for example, research that was conducted while the site was being designed revealed that "very few Web-store sites were delivering a customer experience consistent with what you would expect from a real store,"[6] —from customer service response times to gift wrapping. This discovery prompted Victoria's Secret to form a customer response team dedicated to receiving and servicing feedback from Web shoppers.

There are several ways to approach creating a customer-centric site. Thinking through the Consumption Cycle, analyzing customers' experiences with competitors and other e-commerce sites, conducting market research, and intelligently applying technology should all be part of the creative mix.

Think about visitors' initial, precustomer visits to your site. You want to capture information about visitors and their behavior. However, you must rely on a new visitor's willingness to provide you with information about herself. Once on the site, where does she go? What information is of interest to her? What are her needs? Then, should she become a customer, and her expectations for Web interaction become quite different again, she'll expect you to know and service her in short order.

Technologies for capturing site visitor information have advanced as the commercial Web has matured. There are multiple levels of sophistication available. The simplest technique, known as segmentation, enables visitors to be guided down a path from the site home page by answering a few questions. For instance, are you a software developer? If so, click here. Are you interested in solutions for the banking industry? If so, click there. Through this simple segmentation process, visitors can connect to a series of related pages that target their interests. Their navigational path can be tracked by analyzing the number and order of "hits" (visits to specific pages). This allows companies to make some projections about individuals who are visiting their Web sites and what kind of information they want.

Stages of Site Visitor Data Capture

[segmenting] → [profiling] → [personalization]

The next level of sophistication enables site owners to capture much more detail about visitors to their sites through a practice known as profiling. Onsite registration in the common database is at the heart of profiling. The most basic registration system needs to be flexible (including the ability to augment information in a customer's or prospect's profile), scaleable (the ability to grow and change with the company), and extensible (have the ability to communicate and exchange information with other databases).

Profiling allows the Web system to track a registered user as he navigates through the site. Basic profiling technologies track navigation usage. More sophisticated systems contain comprehensive data about a user's history with the company. For prospects, this may include all visits to the site, their behavior on the site, things they may have downloaded, etc. For companies tracking customers, the profile information should be much more comprehensive. It should access all of their site visit history as well as ongoing business history, such as purchasing and payment information, technical support data, customer service data, and anything else relevant to the customer relationship. It can also contain permissions for user access to proprietary online information.

A word of caution about registration systems and profiling: Sites often contain cumbersome registration systems that can seem tedious and invasive to users. Many people don't want to give personal data just to provide marketing information, although they are more willing to do so when they can get something of perceived value, such as a free sample product. Keep the registration process to a minimum; there may be other opportunities elsewhere in the site to capture additional information.

There have also been instances of data abuse, where user information was sold or licensed to other entities for commercial purposes. This is highly contrary to the Internet's roots, where aggressive selling has always been verboten. As we've mentioned before, in the Web world, the customer is in control. She will quickly opt out if she feels that she's being heavily "sold" or her privacy is being violated.

The next and most sophisticated level of profiling is personalization. In this practice, profile information about a visitor's behavior is used to anticipate and automatically provide additional information in which the visitor *may* be interested. The most popular form of personalized content is the "mypage.com" variety, where a visitor specifies the type of content she's interested in to customize her own personal page on the site. Based on those preferences, the site serves up specifically related data and also presents other data opportunities that relate to the stated preferences.

This level of customization and service is the ultimate goal of a Whole Experience site. The delivery of highly personalized content on user demand embodies the "Market of One" marketing philosophy that has evolved through the late 1990s, in which the corporation directly addresses the personal needs of an individual customer.

An excellent example of a personalized Whole Experience site is Sun Microsystems (*www.sun.com*). Sun, a leading provider of computer hardware and software, is at the forefront of Web business. Not only did Sun develop the now-famous Java programming language, which enables developers to program for ubiquitous platforms (and particularly the Web environment), but it quickly adopted Web technology in order to create one of the premier Web sites in the world.

Sun offers its customers a service called MySun. MySun enables Sun's Web site visitors to screen and target general information, product updates, and other items of news and interest, making a visit to the umbrella *www.sun.com* Web site a faster and more effective experience. Targeted as a high-end service for global, strategic accounts, MySun lets users set up their company's "personal" profile by designating products, applications, and industries in which they're most interested, as well as integrating company-unique information such as sales rep contact information, purchasing policies, negotiated prices, and special configurations. The system will then deliver to the user the most current content on his chosen topics list as well as links in the Sun.com site every time he goes to his MySun page.

Beyond this, MySun uses a technology known as a publishing server to offer links to users from their Web pages to other areas of the Sun.com site. Their user profile data is used by the publishing server to match up profiles and dynamically (in real-time) present other data on the site that relates to the user's stated areas of interest. For example, if a visitor is interested in servers, she may also be offered information on other related topics, such as storage, back-up technology, and server-related software. This kind of convenience approach saves the customer time and may encourage her to make additional purchases from the same source.

Collaborative Content Publishing

So far, we've discussed the fundamental technical components needed to prepare a successful Whole Experience for your Web site visitors. Let's turn now to the content that will actually be published. As with the infrastructure technologies we've already discussed, there is also an investment required in technology to publish the wide breadth and depth of content necessary for a Whole Experience site. Truly progressive companies empower many people within their businesses to contribute content as a natural and routine part of their jobs. Unfortunately, many companies have not yet reached that level of progression.

Content in the traditional sense refers to text, graphics, facts, figures, or any other type of information that might appear as marketing collateral, such as a brochure, spreadsheet, product catalog, document, or report. In the Web context, it extends far beyond marketing information. It includes commerce information, such as price and availability, order tracking, status information, FAQs (frequently asked questions), problem resolution, and other customer service functions.

With most traditional Web sites, content is culled from many departments within an organization and funneled to a Webmaster or Web team. The Webmaster typically gathers together the raw content and technically converts it into Web-ready formats. The process is very similar to the way content for marketing collateral is created. Regardless of who the writer is, there is always somebody in the marketing group whose job is to deal with the printing and production issues.

Web publishing started out by applying this traditional model to a new medium. But this is an inefficient way for various groups within an organization to push their messages and transactions out to their audiences in the time frame customers have come to expect. Concentrating the Web "production" for an entire company into the hands of a small group creates major slowdowns and a greater margin for error as more technical experts and less content experts make editing and scheduling decisions about the release of the data. It's also an inefficient way for various groups within a company to receive information from their customers.

A more progressive and effective approach is the idea of collaborative publishing—permitting various functional areas within the company to post their own data on the site. This approach reduces the Webmaster bottleneck and allows more timely availability of data to site visitors.

To illustrate, let's consider the product marketing function. Product marketing professionals live and breathe the market space of their products. To stay ahead of the game, they must be able to act and react quickly in setting or responding to market conditions. In the Web world, that can mean updating online pricing, offering special incentives or promotions to counter a competitor's actions, launching new product ideas, adjusting product specifications, and myriad other tasks associated with managing a product. With the incredible speed at which markets can change today, product marketers must be empowered to act swiftly when they need to. Waiting for a Webmaster to fit content changes into their information, which is often waiting on a long publishing queue with other departments' content, can mean the difference between successful market timing and losing out on opportunities. Product marketers should be able to go to a content staging area and add or change content themselves in accord with their own sense of urgency. A collaborative publishing system empowers this kind of action and responsiveness.

Just as much as it serves as a pipeline between the company and its customers, collaborative publishing also allows employees to communicate with each other. When the Web becomes the primary communications vehicle, the messaging process must be controlled by the messengers whenever possible, not by an intermediary like a Webmaster.

National Semiconductor, a leading semiconductor manufacturer, provides an interesting example of collaborative publishing through an extranet service it offers its top-tier customers. National offers personalized Web sites to its major accounts, linked via an extranet to its public Web site, to deliver timely, customized information and encourage customers to direct their sales and support inquiries online. These sites are produced and managed by field sales representatives, who are not typically highly technical people. Sales reps remotely manage sites for their accounts from the field by dialing in through a laptop computer and using a Web browser. They can access the system whenever they need to, twenty-four hours a day, seven days a week. The company's interactive marketing department, in order to support the field reps, needs to develop sites for newly authorized customers quickly without having to significantly rework content, look and feel, or application logic. National employs leading edge, easy-to-use Web content application software to automate the entire process and to reduce the need for any involvement by a Webmaster. "Personalization saves time, and that is the one thing that customers can't replace," said Phil Gibson, director of interactive marketing at National Semiconductor. "Allowing our sales force to publish proprietary information on private account pages for each of their key accounts creates a stronger brand for National and a much higher level of service and productivity for our major accounts."[7]

In most cases, a company's existing technology will be too primitive to support a collaborative publishing model. One of the things executives need to advocate is a more sophisticated system by which information is created and made available on the Web site. This key technology decision must be evaluated in terms of its strategic business impact at the highest cross-functional levels in the organization.

To guide the selection process, managers need to develop an understanding of the existing content publishing process as it works within their firm today. Then, they must evaluate the benefits, costs, and potential drawbacks of collaborative publishing. Can existing legacy systems be upgraded to handle a new publishing process? If not, what type of commercial content publishing tools will do the job? What will it take to move existing content into new systems? Is a custom designed system feasible or practical? What can be done now to help relieve the publishing bottleneck? Additionally, what organizational changes need to be set into motion to enable such a system to succeed within the company?

The solution ultimately chosen must be easy to use for both technical and nontechnical employees to be widely adopted. Finally, to ensure quality and consistency across the organization, solutions must be easy to control and manage.

Driving the Experience with Dynamic Content

If collaborative content publishing is the goal, site content should not be static. A static page is much like a single page of a brochure. First and second generation Web sites were composed of a series of static HTML pages (the Web programming language), which were linked into one cohesive group of pages united by a common theme. The content is fixed. Altering it requires a Web programmer or designer to physically adjust the text, images, and HTML code by hand—one page at a time.

Static sites can work for businesses that have a limited amount of content that does not need to be regularly updated. However, they are terrible for businesses that frequently update large volumes of content in order to meet users' e-commerce and service requirements and that want to keep visitor interest with regularly changing content.

Imagine a large corporation with over fifty thousand Web pages of content trying to convert and post that content to its Web site using static HTML. That's exactly what many companies try to do, and it is perhaps the primary reason many Web initiatives have stalled. Not only does the corporation face the rather large task of converting every page into Web-ready code, but when the content needs to be changed, there is no other choice but to alter it page by page.

If those fifty thousand pages could be placed into a database management system that had HTML templates built into it, the content could be easily accessed and updated by any authorized employee within the company. As well, it could be published to the Web in a matter of keystrokes, without having to perform any technical tasks. If you combine the registration database and user profiling to that database management system, you can provide each site visitor with a customized online experience, created automatically without human intervention. This is called dynamic content generation.

A technology known as a document management and publishing application will allow the company's content to be dynamically served to the user upon request. Dynamic content publishing must also have a central database system that assembles content on the fly. This database functionality is sometimes bundled with application solutions. It will deliver a user-customized look and feel of the Web page, delivered in real-time to the recipient via a company defined template embedded into the browser.

Collaborative publishing systems can also be programmed to have internal control systems to help administer the content between the interconnected databases. Specifically, contributors need to have a way to get the content into the system, and there must also be a way to get content out of the system and onto the Internet. There must also be a way to control access—a filter mechanism to specify permissions for who is allowed to add and update that content.

Oracle Corporation, one of the giants in the information technology industry, updated its customer support systems using dynamic, collaborative content generation to produce a personalized Web site experience for its large customer base. "Oracle created an integrated database publishing model," says Sanchez of Oracle. "We commissioned an internal group called the 'Information Architecture Task Force' to help us decide on a content management system that would be best for Oracle. The new system is designed to interconnect many databases within the company into a common Web interface. This type of system is very advantageous for the customer because we can target information to them. We don't waste their time delivering information they don't want to see. Instead, they come and tell us what they want, the kind of person they are, the kind of company they're from, their preferences, their choices, their interests—and we record all that for them. The next time they visit our site, we can deliver tailored information to them."

Dynamic content can also track behavioral profiles of site visitors. It is integral to the page personalization process being adopted for individual company sites and portal sites that we discussed earlier. There are different technical approaches to dynamic profiling and personalization, which should be evaluated and selected based on the business scope of the site and budget considerations.

One approach is called data marking (also known as spidering), where Web pages or other bits of data accessed through the site are stored in a database and tagged with a unique system identification mark so that they can be identified and recorded when they are accessed. The marks are used to track a user's navigation path and are programmed to be associated with other marked data, which can be offered to users based on their navigational behavior. This rigid method can be cumbersome to program and is generally applied to a limited amount of data because of the involved process of marking all data in the database.

Another approach is to use programs that are predesigned to deliver the comprehensive components of a personalized behavior profiling and personalization system. There are commercially available programs that combine functions like database support, high transaction volumes, and integration with existing business systems. Using expert system technologies based on "fuzzy logic"—a technique that attempts to solve problems in ways that resemble human logic—these software products provide sophisticated tools that enable various in-house personnel, like business managers, content editors, and Webmasters, to dynamically control applications from their desktop computers.

There can be substantial financial differences in the choice of these approaches. While a database marking solution could possibly be implemented for as little as $50,000–$75,000, the packaged applications can cost more than that for just the software, with additional installation and customization charges. However, what seems like a more economical approach at first glance is not necessarily the most economical in the long run.

For example, a large Silicon Valley hardware manufacturer undertook a project to redesign its original static-content Web site into a comprehensive Whole Experience site. The hardware manufacturer engaged the services of a leading technology consulting company to assist the effort and decided to use the Java programming language for the "data marking" approach to the project. However, the project parameters were not clearly defined up front. As too many people got involved in the process, the systems started getting very complicated and were not achieving the established site goals. It was taking much longer to reach a "go live" date than had been scheduled.

When the company finally got to a point where it could publicly present its new site, the systems did not perform with the speed or ease that had been intended. By then the consulting company had moved on to another client, leaving very little in-house expertise on a site that had been mostly built by someone else. More expensive Java programming consultants were brought in. In the long run, this company's economical "grow-your-own" system approach ended up costing more money, time, and sweat than purchasing a packaged application that had a somewhat higher price tag (but that also had lots of pre-designed functionality). Moreover, contractor assistance for the packaged applications would have cost about half of the premium price paid for the Java consultants implementing a one-of-a-kind solution.

The moral of the story? What seem like mundane technical details can have a huge impact on strategic initiatives that impact many aspects of a company's ability to effectively service its customers *and* be competitive in its market space. It is very important to start out by carefully defining the goals and parameters for your site development and costing out the entire project in terms of the different possible scenarios that can occur.

ONLINE AUCTIONING MOVES MORE INVENTORY

Another emerging business practice that is born out of dynamic content and the common database is online auctioning. Online auctioning is based on the same principles of traditional auctions—placing bids on items for sale. The new cyber twist is in negotiating price using computers to quickly identify inventory for sale and determining what price the market will bear. Technology is enabling this process to become dynamic. We've already discussed how businesses are becoming savvier about their customers by tracking and analyzing data about their online behavior. Because of the Internet, customers are also becoming savvier by obtaining more information about available products and services, what they cost to manufacture, and what they cost to buy. As more buyers and sellers come together online, relatively inexpensive computer processing power means auction negotiation can be dynamically driven by systems designed to track inventory and cost of goods, which will then instantly calculate acceptable pricing levels.

Auctioning is being put into practice for business-to-business as well as individual consumer transactions. For instance, MBT International (*www.mbtinternational.com*) auctions more than $100 million worth of agricultural products through its site; FreeMarkets OnLine (*www.freemarkets.com*) auctions industrial products and intermediate components. For the individual consumer, there is the enormously popular eBay (*www.ebay.com*), a worldwide White Elephant sale where average people can buy or sell everything from obscure sheet music to sports memorabilia to Mardi Gras beads.

Auctioning is also a highly effective way to move perishable or vanishing inventory (like unused cargo space on an airplane), thereby salvaging otherwise lost revenue. These kinds of added value possibilities should be weighed when evaluating your site technology investment.

Measuring the Effectiveness of Your Site

Now that you've seen the significant technology investment that must be made to develop a successful Whole Experience site, it's crucial to know if that investment is paying off. How do you measure the effectiveness of what you've implemented?

Reporting technologies can help to extract any kind of data that is captured on your site. There are many levels within a typical organization, and reporting should be tailored to everyone's needs. For instance, marketing may want demographic information about site visitors or want to measure site traffic patterns after a special promotional or news announcement. Customer support may want to know how many people are downloading site data that addresses a certain product problem. Finance and accounting departments may want to use all data about recorded financial transactions.

There is myriad information to be gathered about the site experience itself. For instance, which pages on your site are the most requested? Which are least requested? What are the top point-of-entry pages? (This is usually a home page, but it may include others.) What are the pages from which people most often leave your site? Which external sites most frequently refer visitors to your site? Analyzing this data can help you understand the key factors that bring people to your site, make the site engaging, or make visitors lose interest. It can also help you understand which portals or other associated sites (e.g., partner sites and vendor sites) or search engines are most productive for your company and justify continued or increased investment.

You can also gather important feedback about system band-width. Tracking the volume of activity as hits or kilobytes trans-ferred will give you highly measurable data about the activity on your site—what it looks like during normal traffic periods, peak periods, and lulls. You may be able to establish some sense of traffic trends, although, as we've already said, that can be subject to unexpected change at any time on the Web. You can track when client systems have made errors in trying to access your server and when errors have occurred on the server itself. This kind of data is critical to analyzing where you may need to adjust your technical resource investments in order to keep delivering a successful site experience to the customer.

Reporting can be accomplished with out-of-the-box products or custom designed solutions. The right approach depends on the depth of your analytical needs. For instance, if you want simple information, like point-of-site entry or how long a visitor viewed a particular page, many packaged solutions could fit the bill. But if you need feedback on particular functionality that is unique to your business, a custom solution is probably the better way to go. As E-Greeting's Tony Levitan describes it, "We have a wealth of data and a dearth of information. We need to learn how to use information to drive business and relationships with customers. The tools are just emerging and are not ready for prime time. [So] we are building our own."

Roundpeg's Aaron Downey summarizes reportings' strategic importance: "Reporting is going to be a big part of the Web future, because information is King. The more we can gather, the better." Downey sees the eventual possibility of sites being pro-grammed to automatically change and respond based on data captured on a site and the responses and behaviors of site visi-tors—reporting could become an automatic thrust of dynamic content generation. Keep an eye out for it.

Pulling It All Together

We've talked about a lot of different technical elements required for a Whole Experience Web site. It should be very evident by now that this undertaking is a strategic decision that involves careful judgment and long range thinking. While the level of investment may seem daunting, we want to reiterate that it's important to make the commitment and deploy the resources to do it right the first time. With Web commerce developing at lightning speed, cutting corners or waiting too long just may mean the difference between competitive advantage and losing out. Consider this especially when weighing the decision to select packaged applications versus customized systems—version revisions and bug fixes for packaged software are available for purchase according to someone else's schedule, not yours. Make sure you can afford the waiting time that may be required.

Figure 6.1 summarizes the functional framework for a Whole Experience site and the areas of required technology investment that we've been discussing.

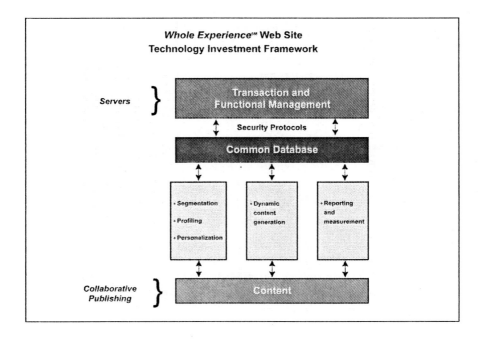

DEFINING THE SITE REQUIREMENTS

Once you have decided on the strategic goals of your system, the next step is to define the details of the system. Whether you intend to build it in-house with your IT staff, outsource it to a Web-development company, or some combination of both, it is vital to clearly document the requirements of the project and the process for moving forward.

A Site Requirements Document is used to clearly state the design, functionality, and business objectives of a Web site. Creating this document will probably involve substantial internal negotiation and discussion about what exactly the site's goals are and how the site will be developed to go about meeting those goals. Keep in mind that this has strategic impact, and business as well as technical strategists should be included in the process. The Site Requirements Document should include details such as:

- A statement of the document's purpose
- A summary of the Web site's objectives
- The strategy planned to meet the objectives (e.g., particular ways the site may be organized, technologies that will be implemented to enable special functionality, etc.)
- An overview of the site navigation framework
- The site's design specifications (e.g., look and feel standards, page construction standards, template requirements, etc.)
- Areas of content (i.e., all of the types of information that will be published on the site and how it will be organized)
- The required technical functionality and its specifications, which may include topics such as:
  Legacy content conversion policies
  Parameters of the registration system, including specific customer information to be captured
  Product entitlement information (who can have access to what)
  Dynamic page generation policies
  Administration and content creation practices
  Search functionality
  Threaded discussions and chat

- Areas of the site for testing purposes, such as pages for alpha and beta content
- Reporting mechanisms

The definition of the site requirements must be thoroughly spelled out in plain language at the beginning of the process so that everyone has a clear understanding of the goal and the framework and can work together in order to achieve it. This site definition should help drive technology and other resource investment decisions that will be required.

Another helpful form, the Request for Proposal, is used to request bids from service organizations who will do the actual design and development work. The service organization may be a department inside your corporate structure or an outside contractor. Either way, building the site will require the commitment of resources, such as money for new technology, access to existing technology infrastructure, staff time, and budget charge-backs to various functional areas. It is vital for the organization that will be doing the work to understand the requirements and expectations so it can properly determine the size and scope of the project and what resources will be needed in order to meet the goals that were finalized in the Site Requirements Document. Some of the content in the Request for Proposal may overlap what is specified in the Site Requirements Document. That's OK, because these two documents are geared toward different audiences. An example of what might appear on a Request for Proposal includes:

- A statement of intent (i.e., the formalized goals for the site)
- Overview of current company operations:
  High-level business overview
  Current systems administration practices
  Company services that require Web integration
  Sales channels that require Web integration
  Back office operations that require Web integration
  Content development roles, responsibilities, and
    processes

- Overview of current system development
  Physical locations of company facilities
  Communication links currently in place
  Current usage patterns
  Expansion plans
- System requirements (brand new and/or integration with
  existing systems)
  General requirements
  E-commerce software
  Additional Web servers
  Publishing software
  Document management
  Databases
  Browsers supported (lowest common denominator)
  Firewalls
  Other Web technologies (e.g., speech recognition, video,
    and audio)
  Special networking considerations (e.g., virtual private
    networks)
  Support
  System administration
- Budget
  Current hardware and software investments that may be
    increased
  Estimated costs associated with site development (licens-
    ing, new technologies and products, labor, maintenance,
    and support costs)
- Timeline
  Alpha test
  Beta test
  Go-live date

DEPLOYMENT

Once these definition processes are complete, development
begins. The length of this phase varies depending on the breadth
of the site's objectives, the volume of work, and the inevitable
unexpected technical glitches. When site development begins to

approach readiness, testing begins. The life cycle for all technology systems includes three testing phases prior to general availability: the alpha test, the beta test, and the usability test. It is vital to conduct all three testing phases before your Whole Experience site "goes live."

The alpha test is the earliest phase of product testing. It is performed by in-house staff only and involves evaluating system design, progress and challenges to date, and fundamental architectural changes that may need to be made. Participants in alpha testing are technical people who understand the possibilities and implications of various technical approaches to reaching the ultimate goal.

Beta testing is performed under normal operating conditions by users who are generally outside of but close to the company (such as members of your distribution channel or key customers). By the time a product or Web site reaches beta testing, it is almost ready to be released. The beta-testing phase can last from a week or two to a few months, depending on the complexity of what is being designed: feedback is provided, bugs are found, code gets revised. Participants in beta testing are generally those who have particular technical expertise or for whom the product or site being developed has some special impact. Beta participants should be chosen carefully, with the number of participants limited to an adequate cross-section to give you meaningful results.

Usability testing is a tricky but vital part of the game. Many companies wait until a product or a Web site is just about to be launched to do final testing with customer-like people. The goal is to let outsiders (who are not necessarily technologically knowledgeable) interact with the product or site and see if they understand what it does, how to use it, and if they are comfortable with the way the experience allows them to perform tasks or reach a goal (such as having a positive Whole Experience). They will also evaluate things like site content and ease of navigation. This kind of feedback is critical to a product's commercial success—it is the same for your Web site.

With some technologies, it may be possible to "tweak" the highest layers of code for necessary adjustments that become evident through usability tests. However, such adjustments can often involve code changes at deeper, more complicated levels— things that should have been thought of during initial design phases. This may not always be possible without significant delays and cost overruns. For that reason, we advocate various phases of usability testing throughout your Web site development cycle. Even if coding is not far enough along at a given time to let the test subjects work with the actual site, site functionality, various pages, links, and interface mechanisms can be demonstrated graphically on paper or through other creative mechanisms. If your company lacks the expertise in conducting this kind of testing, there are research agencies available to facilitate these processes.

Invest with Confidence

We've talked a lot about key functionalities required for a Whole Experience site and the business benefits that can result from them. Having some sense of the many layers of interrelated technology required will hopefully facilitate your investment decisions and the trade-offs that will inevitably need to be made. In the rapidly changing world of Web business, keeping up and meeting customers' expanding expectations can feel like chasing a moving target. Embrace the challenge, for your competitors surely will. Plan carefully, leaving room for growth and flexibility. Ultimately, your investment decisions must be based on the unique requirements and processes of your particular business and what it takes to effectively service and satisfy your customers. But remember that building a Whole Experience site is a strategic decision that will impact business for a long time to come.

Chapter Seven

Internationalize Your Web Strategy and Execution

"Merchants have no country. The mere spot they stand on does not constitute so strong an attachment as that from which they draw their gains."

—Thomas Jefferson

Throughout this book, we've looked at uses of the Web as a strategic business vehicle and the competitive benefits that can be gained by providing your customers with a successful Whole Experience through a well executed Web site. The discussion would not be complete without addressing the importance of internationalization in that execution. To be truly effective and live up to the potential of this global medium and channel, a Web site's strategy and implementation must meet the business and cultural requirements of all the geographic regions within which a company does or intends to do business.

Many readers of this book work for multinational corporations (MNCs)—companies who do business in more than one country. Other readers may start out being focused on only a single country, but by the very nature of establishing a presence on the World Wide Web, may quickly encounter an opportunity to branch out geographically. International customers may find you, or rather, you may decide to adopt a multinational model because the Web offers a cheaper cost of entry and easily enables a global presence.

The decision to become a MNC is a business strategy decision that must be made by each individual company, which is not the subject of this chapter. But once that decision is made, the systems that support the international business—both traditional and technological—must be integrated into the Web context.

Issues like government regulation and taxation of e-commerce are new and relatively undefined. Privacy and security of data collected online are growing concerns. Approaches to these challenges will evolve over a period of years, so how you manage them today may need to be revised six months from now, and six months from then, and then again. In this chapter, we hope only to raise your consciousness about issues that will need to be addressed, and how they can impact the success or failure of your Web effort.

How Much of the World Uses the World Wide Web?

The Web represents an unprecedented opportunity to expand your market size and reach. According to the Global Internet Project (sponsored by the Information Technology Association of America), the number of worldwide Internet users is expected to reach a quarter billion regular users by the year 2000.[1] International Data Corporation, a leading IT industry analyst firm, forecasts the volume of worldwide electronic commerce to reach $425 billion in combined business-to-business and consumer spending by 2002.

The Internet reaches into well over a hundred countries around the world, although the number of users is not evenly distributed on a global basis. The United States, the birthplace of the Internet and a global technology leader, has had the greatest number of Internet users throughout the 1990s and was the first place to begin commercial development of the Web. Other highly industrialized nations, like Japan and those in Western Europe,

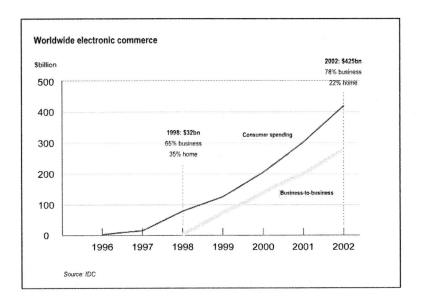

were also among the earliest to begin embracing commercial Web opportunities. But with the enormous growth of computers and particularly PCs (there are estimated to be more than 400 million personal computers in the world), populations of most nations, even lesser developed countries (LDCs), are getting connected to the Internet in growing numbers. While the United States will likely continue to hold the predominant number of users for a single nation in the next several years, user growth in the rest of the world is projected at more than two and a half times that of the United States, with the fastest growth expected in Asia and Pacific Rim countries.

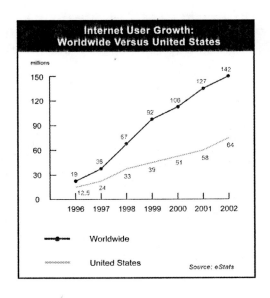

Despite this growth, not every geographic market is equally ready to embrace electronic commerce on a broad scale. Readiness is dependent on multiple issues. For instance, user access to computers and the Internet can vary greatly according to various standards: wealth (How many people have PCs on their desks at work? How about at home?); technology infrastructure (How good is the national or regional phone line system? How many people have gone "wireless"?); cultural issues (Can workers be trusted to get their work done and not spend the day surfing the Net?). In some countries, cost structures for Internet access and telephone charges may be much higher than in others, curbing Web usage. Or the population at large may not be comfortable with technology, particularly as a vehicle for shopping. These are vital issues that may take a while to resolve. Factoring these conditions into your analysis will guide you regarding how to prioritize your Web investment. Then you can better determine how to concentrate and prioritize your Web effort in market territories that are the most technologically ready.

Ken Orton explains the conditions that sparked dramatic growth of the Web in the United States and what is expected in Europe: "The online market in the United States caught fire. It caught fire because of the economy, and it caught fire because of companies like AOL. There was a perfect blend of conditions, which contributed to the explosive growth of Internet usage in the United States" Preview anticipates the European market's eventual readiness for explosive growth in Web usage and is planning expansion there. "Preview Travel will soon launch our service in the European market. I believe that it will have a much faster acceptance than what we experienced in the United States. The European market is preconditioned—they already have access to many of the United States e-commerce brands, with more coming online everyday. The French may find it easy to transition from their existing Minitel service to an Internet service. The Scandinavian countries are starting to see really heavy online penetration, both at work and at home. Germany now has over 4 million online households, and the industry is investing heavily in the country's technology infrastructure."

Autobytel.com also anticipates major international expansion opportunities through licensing agreements and relationships with partners and dealers in foreign markets. Its multinational network encompasses Canada, the United Kingdom, and Scandinavia, with further targets throughout Europe and possibly beyond as more desirable markets for automobiles also become more desirable technologically.

The readiness factors unique to each market sector and geography must be taken into account to guide an international Web expansion that will capitalize on opportunity and deliver the best return on investment to meet your overall objectives.

Considerations for Internationalizing a Whole Experience Site

There are some special considerations in implementing an effective Whole Experience on an international basis. In addition to all of the topics we've already explored throughout this book, internationalizing your Web site involves a skillful blending of general business expertise along with an understanding of localized market characteristics, such as legal and tax regulations and infrastructural and cultural realities, which can vary greatly from country to country. In the following pages, we'll explore considerations that are unique to internationalized e-commerce.

LOCALIZED CONTENT

Localizing content is a fundamental step in effectively internationalizing a Web presence. Localization involves converting your site from the language, functional, cultural, and presentation requirements of one market into those of another. Just as with localizing printed materials, products, or services, Web site localization demonstrates your commitment to an international market because you have put in the effort to show that you are sensitive to its unique cultural and business environment. Specific considerations for localizing a Web site include choice of geographic markets for which you will localize, creation or conversion of content relevant to the local market in the local language, business and cultural practices in those markets, and back-end process issues such as databases, online applications and forms, and e-mail.

N2K, Inc., a music entertainment company using the Internet as a global platform for promoting, marketing, and selling music and music-related merchandise (now merged with CDNow), launched Japanese versions of Music Boulevard (*www.music-blvd.com/jp*) and Jazz Central Station (*www.jp.jazzcentral-station.com*). By forming alliances with local fulfillment operations, the company expanded the number of titles offered and provided more localized product to international markets. The company also formed an agreement with MTV Networks to create localized MTVMusic Boulevard sites for Europe, Brazil, Japan, and other Asian countries. In addition, they offered registration and ordering instructions on Music Boulevard in German, French, Japanese, Spanish, and English.

"The best approach to Web site localization is to first identify those areas most critical to your business goals," says Deborah Tyroler, Senior Web Strategist at International Communications (*www.intl.com*), a multilingual solutions provider. "Determining how you want to target your international customer will help you to define the formation and foundation of a localization plan. You'll need to set priorities with respect to content and to target markets. For example, if products and services will vary from market to market, you will want to reflect this in your site by customizing the content. Even if the content remains ostensibly the same, local tastes, preferences, and conventions may influence how you position products or services. You may only need to provide some basic translated marketing materials to draw the international visitor into the site. On the other hand, it may be integral to the site that you allow for multilingual online ordering capabilities and e-mail interaction. The key to designing a successful and effective multilingual site is to assess and prioritize around creating a positive online experience for users worldwide."

The ideal situation is to build multinational capabilities into your site from the beginning. If you are already a MNC, or know up front that you will use the Web to expand into global markets, you can plan and design your site to be multinational and more easily localized. Tyroler emphasizes that structure, aesthetics, and content are equally important both to ensure that a Web site will work visually and functionally for users worldwide and to maximize the site's value for both user and host. For those who are "retrofitting" localization into existing sites, challenges like navigation redesign are not necessarily practical, so localization should emphasize content and functionality. You will want to maintain brand consistency in look and feel from your home site to your international sites, but you may need to modify the exact content. Make sure that the content you do select is relevant to the market you're addressing and fits into local access parameters like bandwidth, phone connection charges, etc. A word-for-word or image-for-image translation may not be the right thing to do.

For instance, sites with lots of slick graphics may work well in some countries, but they may not work in others where entertainment value is a much lower priority than quickly finding needed information; thus, long page loading times would be frustrating. Plan for these kinds of limitations early so that your investment in the corporate home site can be maximized across all regional sites as you expand. Be sure to get help from in-country advisors, such as overseas staff or consultants, on how things are done on the local level.

"Lasting impressions are made in the presales experience," says International Communications's Tyroler. "When international Web users arrive at your site and find information in their own language, they feel an immediate connection to your product. They know you are committed to their local market. Everything they need is right there, and a purchase decision is an impulse away."[2]

TECHNOLOGY INFRASTRUCTURE TO SUPPORT LOCALIZED SITES

Technical infrastructure for sites takes on another level of complexity when you internationalize. Some companies are displaying corporate-, country-, or region-specific navigation options on their main home page. This approach gives site visitors the option to choose which language or which country's information they want to access. There are several ways, from a technical infrastructure perspective, to accomplish this. One central site can accommodate the full range of geographic content. Another way to accomplish a localized experience is to replicate the home site's content and functionality through different sites set up on servers dedicated to a particular country or region. While this duplication of IT infrastructure is an added expense, it can greatly facilitate international e-commerce in several ways. As we already mentioned in chapter 6, local servers can enhance response time for site visitors and help ensure a smooth performance through differing peak traffic periods. Also, having a separately hosted site that is accessible from within a given country—and which contains information specific to that country—is a way to more easily comply with country-specific laws and regulations about e-commerce site content and the posting of data that is unique to one given region, such as pricing or product line availability.

Let's look at an example of how a company is approaching this: Cisco Connection Online (CCO) offers a comprehensive range of globalization features to meet the needs of its worldwide audience. In addition to English, CCO users can navigate, access indexes, and obtain help in fourteen other languages. Local content is available for forty-nine countries. Users have site access to regionally located site servers for streamlined country-specific connections to mission-critical information and networked applications. Cisco has installed three remote distribution servers with local points of presence (POPs) in countries throughout the world. While Cisco dictates corporate look-and-feel standards on a worldwide basis, regional business partners can customize their country-specific pages based on local laws, customer sets, and marketing campaigns. By providing corporate guidelines as well as local flexibility, Cisco is able to ensure brand continuity across all of its markets while accommodating the unique needs of its worldwide customers.

"A global networked business spans all geographies, fostering close relationships with customers, partners, prospects, suppliers, and employees worldwide," says Sinton of Cisco Connection. "CCO's globalization features demonstrate how companies can leverage the power of networking to streamline business processes and improve access to critical information and resources on a truly global scale." Cisco's model encompasses:

- Servers: Cisco has installed CCO remote distribution servers with local POPs in countries throughout the world. Users can now access all CCO guest services—including product information, documentation, and technical tips—through dedicated links in forty-nine companies. Selecting a country-specific server will take you to that regional server, where you will be able to access up-to-date guest information and services.
- Languages: Translated versions of the CCO home page and many other key CCO pages are available in fourteen languages: Chinese, Danish, Dutch, Finnish, French, German, Italian, Japanese, Korean, Norwegian, Portuguese, Russian, Spanish, and Swedish. Hundreds of additional translated documents, including press releases, are also available.
- Countries: Cisco has developed forty-nine "country pages" that display information specific to both country and region, such as local Cisco offices, service and support contacts, certified sales and support partners, seminars, events, and training courses.
- Culture: Cisco allows each regional partner to customize its "country pages" based on local laws, customs, and marketing campaigns. Cisco recognizes that individual sites must reflect the local values of the targeted region.

By providing a consistent user interface and integrated regional access worldwide, Cisco is further extending the Whole Experience business model that has made CCO the premier example of the right way to do business over the Internet. CCO's globalization features demonstrate how companies can use the power of networking to streamline business processes and improve access to information and resources on a truly global scale.

Dell Computer is also aggressively adopting a localization strategy. Dell's Web site is up and running in twenty-one different languages in fifty-eight different countries. According to Dell's Robert Langer, "We're probably doing about 25–30 percent of our total revenue overseas. Through our online efforts, we've been conducting business internationally for quite some time now. We have distributors in all the major countries and certain smaller countries where our business is still pretty young. But over time, the plan is always to replace local distributors with a direct operation."

Symantec is another company on the leading edge of localization. Symantec has organized its site as hubs of content broken down by different foreign territories. Each offers essentially the same services but is truly local in content and language. The company maintains twelve regional e-commerce hubs, with the back-end infrastructure supported globally by an internal e-commerce organization. The power of this approach is that sales strategies and customer interaction are localized and locally supported.

LEGAL AND ETHICAL CONSIDERATIONS

Legalities and ethics vary widely from country to country. Trying to police a pervasive, invasive, and polymorphous sociological phenomenon like the Web is a challenge that has governments concerned, frustrated, and at times even conflicted. There are as many ways to look at legal and ethical issues as there are countries in the world and differing political and social groups within those countries. While the Web can bring the world closer together, its newness, unfamiliarity, and unbounded potential cause many governments—and often individual citizens—to approach it with caution.

Web commerce brings an entirely new dimension to doing business across borders. Traditionally, many governments impose restrictions on what kinds of products can be sent or received from outside national boundaries. For instance, the U.S. government had, for many years, very strict controls that did not allow shipments of U.S. technical goods and services to enter any part of the former Soviet Union. Restrictions on the physical delivery of goods to other countries is one of the issues to be weighed in your decision to become a MNC. But suppose you are selling intangible goods that can be delivered electronically over the Internet. Most governments would have great difficulty knowing about that, let alone monitoring it. This premise holds true in pretty much all countries with free access to telephony, Internet, and other communication vehicles. Although, if you consider countries that have very strong central governments, that may not be the case.

In China, for example, a considerable volume of Internet traffic is passed through government gateways, which may be randomly monitored for legality and acceptability. This practice affects obvious e-commerce transactions that involve intangible as well as physical goods. However, there are products that can become culturally impermissible, depending on the standards of the current administration. Kennedy A. Brooks, an attorney and currently executive vice president of global planning and development for NETEQ Corporation, an international Web strategy and development company, says that while business-to-business communications in this market are not usually problematic, business-to-consumer communications can be tricky if the publisher of the Web content is not up on local laws and mores.[3] However, Brooks notes that China is a huge burgeoning market with a good Internet technology backbone, which can certainly be worth the extra accommodations that will undoubtedly be required. As with any localization effort, do your research before heading into this or any foreign market. When possible, program restrictions by product and country into your online ordering systems for automatic screening of electronic orders that may be prohibited. Preview Travel, for example, automatically screens ticket purchases originating from outside the United States if the ticket holder leaves from and returns to a non-U.S. destination.

Another area that is causing rapidly rising concern is the use of customer information gathered online. In the United States, information about customers is gathered in huge volumes as a matter of course. It is used for research, marketing, customer service, and historical record keeping. It is also sometimes sold to other entities for marketing purposes. While the average consumer may not always like that situation, these practices are for the most part legal and considered within the bounds of business ethics.

The Web has added a new element to the process of customer data collection with the emergence of online site registration and customer profiling, as we discussed earlier in this book. While perhaps legal in the United States, customers are increasingly concerned about how the data is being used and irritated at being required to provide it. And, outside the United States, the practice may not only be socially unpalatable, it may even be unlawful. For instance, in European Union (EU) member countries, a regulation called the EU Data Directive prevents the transfer of information to countries that do not adhere to the EU's strict rules of privacy protection. This can pose a real problem to MNCs, particularly those outside of the EU, that may be trying to service customers in different countries. This legal issue is impacting the way Web business practices are evolving in EU and non-EU countries.

Web site content is another area of huge legal and ethical debate. Concerns range from availability of violent or pornographic material to aggressive marketing techniques. What is perceived as offending material can vary greatly by country. Take, for example, an American institution—the Walt Disney Company. While many parents and children may consider the Disney.com site to be wholesome family entertainment, the site has caused an uproar in Denmark. Hagen Joergensen, Denmark's National Consumer Ombudsman, considers the site to be threatening to Danish children because he feels its focus is too marketing-oriented. Aggressive marketing to children is prohibited in Denmark under the Danish Marketing Practices Act. A series of disagreeable communiqués between Mr. Joergensen and Disney finally escalated to the front page of the *Wall Street Journal*.[4] Disney does not have any entertainment properties in Denmark, so prior to the emergence of the Web, this kind of conflict could not have been an issue. Even though Denmark is not the biggest market Disney targets, this disagreement created, nonetheless, an unpleasant public relations situation that garnered international attention.

With all of these perceived risks being associated with Web commerce and the Internet, there is a growing move for protection and regulation—but what kind? Governments in many countries are considering the possibility of imposing regulations, varying from privacy policies to taxation. The imposition of traditional regulatory mechanisms is an instinctual, natural inclination and helps preserve the idea of national sovereignty and the protection of one's borders and institutions. But enforcing regulations on Web business—which has by nature developed as borderless—will be difficult and expensive to police. The entire concept of the open boundaries of Web business is a radical new social paradigm, and there are strong supporters on both sides of the issue—some advocating market self-regulation and others advocating government involvement.

The EU Data Directive we previously mentioned is one example of a government intervention that is already impacting the development of Web commerce. By preventing the transfer of customer data to countries that don't meet EU-defined privacy standards, the EU is providing a level of protection to its own citizens, but is inhibiting what many perceive as an essential business process involving free trade with other countries. As the EU grows in strength as an economic entity, many corporations in non-EU countries are starting to see issues like the Directive as an inhibitor to trade and hope to stem further regulations in Europe and elsewhere by proposing market self-governance. For instance, leaders from large multinational corporations, including IBM, Time Warner, Fujitsu Ltd., Toshiba, France Telecom SA, and others, formed a coalition called the Global Business Dialogue on E-Commerce to take a leadership position on industry self-regulation. They are focused on proposing strategies and policies for privacy, taxation, and security, and particularly, on finding ways to coexist with or influence the implementation of the EU Directive to facilitate trade within that region.

Other organizations, such as the nonprofit group TRUSTe, are also working to lead in the field of self-regulation. TRUSTe defines Internet privacy guidelines and licenses or certifies commercial Web sites that are in compliance with them. Consortia such as the Global Internet Project and the Privacy Partnership Campaign (cosponsored by TRUSTe) have also formed to pursue the same basic goals. Despite this growing movement, there are many who contend that commercial entities cannot be trusted to regulate themselves for the adequate protection of consumers and compliance with laws. The entire issue of Web regulation is a key area to watch, as it can potentially have a major impact on how and where companies target their Web-commerce efforts. The added administrative requirements that may be imposed by such regulations could also potentially create a burden sufficient to prohibit smaller companies from enjoying the equal player status enabled by the Web to date. E-commerce companies can best prepare themselves by learning about the legal and ethical standards in countries where they intend to conduct trade and then establishing fair Web practices that respect those standards.

TAXATION

In the same vein as regulation, taxation of Web commerce is another area where governments are trying to analyze and establish their role. This area is still largely undefined, as the accelerated pace of the Internet greatly exceeds that at which traditional government processes, like deciding upon tax legislation, normally work.

Based on our research, there is some good news on the tax question, in that most of the leading economically developed countries that are evaluating this issue realize the potential of the Internet to revolutionize and greatly hasten the development of global commerce. There is a consciousness among industry groups, think tanks, and governments of the need to keep this channel of trade as uncomplicated as possible in order to encourage and stimulate global trade while maintaining a fair and predictable tax system that generates revenue. That being said, the reality of what an individual government actually does can vary

greatly, depending on times of prosperity or necessity and pre-
vailing political conditions.

Traditional, tangible goods purchased online but physically
delivered across borders will still be subject to the normal customs and duty collection processes of a given country. Many have
Value Added Tax (VAT) already built into the online price, if VAT
is a normal part of the national tax system. But the biggest challenges lie in the area of digitally delivered goods and services.
Since the delivery of these kinds of products (predominantly software, data and information, music, travel services, finance and
brokerage services, and entertainment) is intangible, tracking and
reporting is, for the most part, left to the honesty of the seller,
under the most current set of governmental practices and rules.
These rules are coming under scrutiny by governments the world
over to see how they might need to be revised for e-commerce. It
is likely that stricter reporting and auditing processes will result.
But the modification of such rules to encourage honesty under
existing tax requirements does not necessarily mean that a new,
additional layer of taxes will result. In fact, there is a large push in
many countries against this kind of discriminatory Web taxation.

In the United States, the Clinton administration has been
very forthcoming in its support of the Web as a place for free
trade. Through its 1997 "Framework for Global Electronic Commerce" the administration recommended the establishment of a
duty-free zone for electronically delivered products and services.[5]
After political wranglings, a two-year tax moratorium on Internet
access and commerce finally made it through Congress in 1998.
While two years isn't very long, it does provide enough time to
see how the Web channel is developing, to study what some of
the taxation benefits and challenges might be, and, if taxation is
imposed, to develop a more reasonable and proactive approach
that does not hinder the greater economic benefits of Web commerce. This issue will undoubtedly have at least some bearing on
the next major U.S. election.

Even with strict privacy initiatives, such as the EU Directive
we discussed earlier, the European Commission is also recognizing the need for moderation on the tax issue. A June 1998 *Global*

Tax News report, which was issued by the international consulting firm KPMG, quoted EU Tax Commissioner Mario Monti as stating that solutions were needed, "in cooperation with all interested parties at the Community and international level, so that the tax system does not impede the development of this highly promising sector."[6]

The Organization of Economic Cooperation and Development (OECD), a think tank consisting of members from twenty-nine countries, is a leading international group that works to understand and influence policy issues, including e-commerce taxation, pricing, customs, and royalties issues, among many others. This organization, which includes some highly influential individuals and leading edge thinkers, has been very actively working to explore and propose solutions for these developing Web challenges in ways that will be fair to all parties and that will continue to stimulate global commerce. Through these kinds of groups, the Web is instigating international participation and problem solving in ways never before required or probably even considered.

While federally governing laws are one (usually dominant) force in imposing trade regulations, another complexity in the system can be "subnational governments." These primarily include state or provincial and city or county governments. These entities may attempt to impose additional tax requirements on e-commerce that can conflict with and/or greatly complicate national tax systems. For instance, the U.S. government decision in favor of a two-year moratorium on Web taxation was considered by some to be a violation of the sovereignty and right of states to impose taxes. That kind of argument goes back to the earliest days of the United States and the intentions of the authors of the U.S. Constitution.

Kennedy Brooks of NETEQ Corporation summarizes his view of the current tax conundrum: "Although it can be argued with some logical and legal foundation that there is nothing fundamentally different about taxation of e-commerce transactions, and therefore existing tax frameworks should suffice, it is almost certain that operational loopholes in present tax laws, and the technical incapacity of many tax collectors to track, and therefore to compel accurate reporting of taxable transactions, will drive governmental authorities (at all levels in the United States *and* throughout the world) to push back against the 'no Internet-specific taxes' position that the Clinton administration has articulated. This is an area of continuing interest."

The issue of which set of laws may be applicable in any given e-commerce situation (or many other legal and tax situations) is known as jurisdiction—whose law applies to a particular transaction? Jurisdiction has traditionally been determined by the location of a "fixed place of business," which can be extremely difficult to enforce with e-commerce, particularly with multinational transactions. However, governments, by nature, will try to maintain sovereignty, even if their rulings are unenforceable in practice. One such mechanism they can employ is a doctrine known as "long-arm jurisdiction." There was an interesting e-commerce case in the state of Minnesota in 1998. In *Minnesota vs. Granite Gate Resorts,* a U.S. gambling service with servers resident in the country of Belize was found in violation of Minnesota antigambling laws by the State Supreme Court because Minnesota residents were gambling online via this service. The court found that because the gambling service was intending to serve customers in the Minnesota market, and because sufficient "minimum contacts" had occurred, Minnesota could establish jurisdiction over the service in its courts. Of course, as NETEQ's Brooks points out, the practical enforcement of an enjoinment against a service provider outside of Minnesota is very difficult to enforce, but it can still have unwelcome legal effects.

While governments in one country or province may not be able to impose their laws on citizens in another, the bigger risk is that of observed patterns of repeated abuse, or behavior that is not government sanctioned, being legislated into restrictions on ISPs and what Web access they may enable. That would truly put a crimp in the open character of the Web and hopefully will not come to be implemented.

There is obviously a strong need for cooperation among countries and subnational governments to keep tax and legal systems as simplistic as possible in order to reach the potential of global commerce through the Web. This will be an enormous challenge. Groups such as the OECD are exploring possibilities for internationally acceptable guidelines for digital "signatures," which could be considered acceptable evidence of identity and origin of transactions for government purposes. Other approaches, such as developing internationally compatible information requirements and data formats, access to third-party information, and cooperative arrangements for tax collection are also being explored. This entire discipline is subject to enormous interpretation and change in the coming years. NETEQ's Brooks encourages concerned business executives (like readers of this book) to participate in the policy process by affiliating with organizations that are working to understand the issues, adopting positions, and making recommendations to governments. Many of these can be found through the Web. In any event, this is a very important issue to watch closely—with the help of a techno-savvy tax professional!

THE END OF LIST PRICING?

Establishing a list price has been practiced throughout the modern era of formalized commerce. As multinational business has accelerated over the last two decades, thanks in large part to advances in technology, vendors and manufacturers have frequently set different price levels for the same product in different geographic markets. Sometimes this has been for tangible reasons—it costs more to set up operations in country X, translating products into a different language increases cost of goods, etc. But in other situations, pricing is just tied to "what the market will bear"—supply and demand based on availability or desirability of products.

The Web is changing that; because of the Web, customers now have much more access to and knowledge about comparative pricing data. Posted pricing for one geographic market cannot be hidden from other geographic markets. There must be very strong and regionally acceptable reasons why one market region would pay more for a product than another region, particularly when you add the burden of shipping and taxation charges to the purchase price. This can work in the favor of some markets and against others. Take, for example, the online purchasing of books in France. Ruthanne Feinberg, manager of the electronic commerce division of the French Trade Commission in San Francisco (part of the French Embassy), says that it is often cheaper for a French customer to purchase books online from a U.S. company and pay the shipping and duty for them than it would be to buy the same titles in France.[7] This is obviously good news for U.S. booksellers like Amazon.com. But if we look at something like U.S.-published software products, American companies have traditionally set international prices for software higher than domestic prices, even without having localized the software. The ability for a French software purchaser to compare pricing on the Web and see what is being charged in other countries will undoubtedly pressure the software publisher toward greater pricing parity throughout its market.

The pricing issue also has sales channel implications. Customers can now more easily look into alternative sources, including purchasing products from other distributors, which may offer a better deal, or buying direct from the manufacturer, if the company happens to take orders online.

Some companies are trying to work with the pricing challenge through the locally hosted site approach we've already mentioned. Giving customers a language-friendly, business-familiar Web experience should help keep them focused on the information a vendor wants to give its particular market, including pricing. But as customers are growing more savvy, there is nothing keeping them from searching the Web for other sites from the same vendor to do a little comparison shopping. They undoubtedly will start to object if differences are unjustifiably too great. Overcoming this business barrier is one of the key challenges to successful multinational e-business. We believe this kind of economic pressure will considerably effect pricing for substitutable goods and will ultimately drive the need for a different pricing model.

In fact, some companies are already adopting new pricing models. As mentioned in chapter 3, online auctions are becoming more popular for reaching a price that will be considered fair and acceptable to buyer and seller, regardless of where they are. Taking that idea a step further, companies like Priceline.com let customers state what they want to buy and what they're willing to pay. Vendors can then offer different product options that may meet customers' stated criteria. Still other companies are experimenting with the idea of pricing that is dynamically matched to customer demand under varying market conditions. For example, ordering a pizza online at noon, at peak traffic time, might cost a customer more than ordering a pizza at three in the afternoon, a lower traffic time. This simple example could be applied on a broader, international scale according to influences such as seasonal product availability, promotional requirements, or other market factors affecting supply and demand. U.S.–based Forrester Research describes this model as part of a new trend toward "dynamic trading," which takes advantage of the Web as a commerce vehicle but requires well-structured, sophisticated technologies in order to execute.

Extending Your Market Reach via the Web

Just because you extend your Web presence into other countries doesn't mean customers will know you're there. While the Web can be an excellent vehicle for breaking into new markets, awareness and lead generation activities must be conducted if you intend to truly develop a market's potential for your products. But the unique nature of the Web puts a different twist on traditional market penetration efforts.

For instance, some companies become multinational quite unexpectedly through their Web presence. One interesting example is Lehigh Valley Safety Shoes, a small company in Pennsylvania. This manufacturer's representative of quality Lehigh Safety Shoes had a local, direct sales presence but decided to put up a Web site to expand its channel strategy. Using some leading edge Web storefront software, Lehigh went live with its site and got itself listed on a few search engines. According to Jim Codrea, Lehigh's Controller and one of the company's three co-owners, the company received its first online order within one month—from Indonesia![8] Lehigh had not intended to do business outside of the United States, but, since the initial order came in, the company has also received orders from Korea, China, and the Philippines. Although aggressive international growth is not part of its current strategy, Lehigh still welcomes overseas sales.

Becoming an "accidental MNC" is one of the effects of putting out your shingle on the Web. For some companies, it invites a market expansion opportunity that hadn't been previously considered but is then decided to be pursued more formally. Others make the choice to decline the opportunity. As we've said, that decision must be made in the context of your overall business strategy. But if you choose the Web as a path to getting there, it will take effort and resources to reach its potential. As Lehigh's Codrea comments, "The biggest thing I didn't think about with regard to the Internet was that it's just like another division—you have to manage it."

Of course, if your strategy is to target development in international markets, then you have to institute formalized awareness and lead generation programs on a country-by-country basis. For those who are already MNCs, a good start is to educate existing customers about the newly localized online resources you're providing them and to lead them to the localized site. But finding new customers takes broader visibility. Internet users worldwide who have English skills often make use of the popular U.S.-based portals for Web searching. Some of these portals, like Yahoo! are localizing for foreign markets. But businesses within different countries are also developing their own portals unique to their local markets. In Latin America, for example, the most popular information sites are Adnet (*www.adnet.com.mx*) and StarMedia (*www.starmedia.com.mx*). The content of these portals is entirely in Spanish (with a second choice of Portuguese on the StarMedia site) and is targeted entirely to the Latin American marketplace. These might be key sites for placing banner ads or listing in

search engines if you want to address the growing Latin
American market with business-to-consumer products. Business-
to-business e-commerce, however, requires a different approach.
According to Ricardo Garcia Zetina, director of marketing and
channels for Centura Software de Mexico, the most popular use
of the Internet in Latin American business at this time is e-mail.[9]
Companies are not only using e-mail to improve communications
with their existing customers, they are also using it in the same
way as hard copy direct mail to obtain new customers. Databases
of e-mail lists are being sold commercially just like databases of
physical address lists. In the United States, this kind of practice,
which produces junk e-mail known pejoratively as SPAM (the
action itself termed "spamming"), is held in contempt. But, in
Latin America, it is more acceptable.

Garcia Zetina also mentions that Latin American perceptions
about Internet security are a major obstacle to using the Web for
anything more than information. So, while a Web presence is
now an important information source in Latin America, a more
traditional approach is better for actual selling, until that market
is infrastructurally and culturally more ready for Whole Experience e-commerce. These kinds of issues will be unique market by
market, so it's important to understand them in context before
taking your Web effort to specific locales.

Penetrating the U.S. Market

Many companies throughout the world are interested in entering
the U.S. market. The Web offers an easier way to approach this
complex marketplace than ever before. Targeting the U.S. market
is a tricky proposition. Americans on the whole love foreign
goods. We are a diverse culture by heritage and are open to trying products offered from just about anywhere. However, this is
an extremely difficult market in which to do business. Many non-
U.S. companies do not understand what entering this market
requires and experience frustration, culture shock, and even failure when not properly prepared.

At this point, for any non-U.S. companies hoping to penetrate the U.S. market, having a Web site is an absolute minimum

requirement. The Internet and the commercial Web were born in the United States, and American expectations for Web access and Web sites are high. U.S. businesspeople frequently use the Web throughout the workday. Home use is also very common. The Web is assuming a major role in almost any market strategy, and URLs are seen everywhere, driving traffic to an ever-growing number of sites.

Non-U.S. Web sites, then, must meet at least minimum standards of expectations to be effective in the U.S. marketplace. Issues as basic as correct spelling and grammar can often be overlooked. Speed, visual appeal, and navigational structure are important as well. Non-U.S. site builders must try to address the nuances and sophistication of the marketing style to which Americans are accustomed. And, U.S. consumer protection laws can be complex and extremely foreign in concept and philosophy to those not raised in our highly regulated society. Incorporating all of this into a Web site can be a tall order to fill, and the effort should not be underestimated.

Ruthanne Feinberg of the French Trade Commission works with French companies trying to penetrate the U.S. market through the Web. Her advice: "You cannot enter the American market without the help of Americans. You must have someone local to help you understand how this large and diverse market works." As sources of help, Feinberg recommends contacting the trade office or consulate of a specific country within the United States, who may be able to offer assistance or recommend other locals who can. In making your evaluation, Feinberg also suggests doing extensive Web research, identifying and understanding what competitors can be found on the Web, and associating with a U.S. company or brand that is visible and known on the Web. A local partner that knows the rules and the realities will always provide an added advantage, whatever country you're in.

Regardless of where you are, when you choose to develop a Web presence you must make a business decision as to whether or not you will be a multinational company. You can't hide from it on the Web, but you can choose to limit your scope, not participate, or bound eagerly after seemingly endless opportunity. The decision to become multinational will certainly bring with it a new set of responsibilities and challenges that are unique to this highly experimental yet very exciting time. If you do choose the MNC path, remember that customers the world over will eventually come to expect a Whole Experience Web site. Building it early will bring you competitive advantage and show your leadership position in the global Web arena.

Chapter Eight

Whole Experience Strategy Road Map

"When written in Chinese, the word 'crisis' is composed of two charac-
ters. One represents danger, and the other represents opportunity."

—John F. Kennedy

This book grew out of the
need to define and help
resolve the key challenges
all companies face as the
Internet becomes an integral part of doing business. Through
Cognitiative's work with clients, we have designed tools to assist
them in creating and implementing their Web strategies. One of
our key tools is the Whole Experience road map, which we use to
help guide clients through their Web strategy development.

This chapter presents our Whole Experience road map and
discusses the actions a company should take along the way in
creating the strategic plan for its Web business. While every
company is different, there are many emerging "best practices"
from which any company can benefit, in terms of the decisions
that must be made to have a successful strategy. There are some
unique elements about developing a Web business strategy that
require new planning processes to transform business strategies
into functional and technical specifications.

Keep in mind that the premise of this book has been to discuss what the customer requires from a company's Web site, how this affects the Web business strategy a company takes, and the trickledown impact this has on many elements of a business. There is another aspect to the Web business strategy that we have only lightly touched upon, as it goes well beyond the topic of a singular book: how to achieve supply chain and operational efficiencies through the deployment of Internet technologies. These are certainly related concepts and, in fact, the business strategy and technology solutions for customer facing and supply chain management should be integrated and leveraged. We believe that the strategic process, however, should begin with understanding the customer and market requirements, as this understanding should drive the internal decisions in supply chain management. But we want to state for the record that companies should be concurrently thinking about the supply and internal operations requirements as part of the broader challenge. The Internet is more than a storefront. When making decisions about strategy and technology solutions, companies need to be thinking much more broadly about the benefits that e-business can bring to the company, in all aspects of its operations.

How to Use This Chapter

Use this chapter as a guide and a reality check to ensure that your company is considering all the key aspects of creating and executing your Web strategy. If you already have begun implementing a Web presence, the guide can be useful as a catalyst for continuous process improvement.

The Whole Experience road map has eight basic phases, which are depicted in figure 8.1. The remainder of this chapter discusses each individual step in terms of data required, the decisions that must be made at that point in the road map, and the output that is required to move onto the next phase. The eight steps of the Whole Experience road map are:

1. Opportunity analysis
2. Business strategy development
3. Functional strategy development
4. Technical specifications
5. Prototype development
6. Site development
7. Operational implementation
8. Ongoing refinement

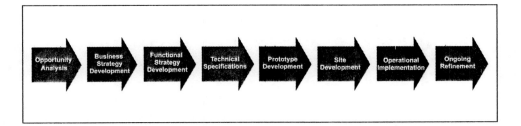

One cautionary note: This road map has many steps and at the outset appears to require many months, if not years, to execute. But we can say with confidence that you do not have that much time; the Web world moves at a faster pace than many companies are accustomed to. We encourage you to set up processes and empower the responsible teams with the goal of ensuring rapid, while thorough, progress.

Step One: Opportunity Analysis

Many companies have determined that they must seriously embrace the Web as a strategic business vehicle, but they are often basing that decision on intuition, perceived market pressures, or anecdotal customer demands. All three of these are part of the decision process, but fully assessing the situation and potential opportunity is a critical step that must be approached with a systematic methodology, not just intuition and one-off data points.

To institute some rigor into the process, a company should create a SWAT team–style task force charged with assessing the opportunity. This team must comprise senior executive management and not be relegated only to middle- and lower-level managers. This task force would be responsible for creating the recommendations on how the company should move forward on a Web strategy. The team members must be people who have direct experience and insight into the company's top-level business challenges, directions, strengths, and weaknesses. And they must be people who have the respect of their superiors, their peers, and the troops, because their recommendations will be the guiding light for the Web strategy.

Data Required

Once the opportunity assessment team is formed, chartering the group with gathering accurate, timely, and insightful market information is the first step. The fundamental questions, with regard to external data, that must be factored into the opportunity analysis include:

- What are competitors offering your target prospects and customers via a Web strategy, and how well are those site experiences meeting the needs of the customer?
- Where are your customers and prospects in the adoption of the Web (i.e., Do they have access to the Web? What do they use it for? How and why do they use it? What are their online behaviors and preferences?)? It is useful to know their preferences even for areas that are not directly related to your relationship with them since these can provide some helpful tips when developing your strategy.
- Do customers want you to offer them a Web alternative to doing business with you? Specifically, which parts of the Consumption Cycle do customers want you to address: shopping, buying, delivery, service, support, or all of the above?

- What is your distribution pipeline doing on the Web? Do your customers currently have Web access to your products via your channels? Is that working well, or is there room for improvement?
- What do your channel partners want you to do regarding the Web?
- What business process improvements and cost savings can be achieved via the Web?

The external data gathered should be compiled in a formal report that will be reviewed as a part of the recommendations from the opportunity analysis team. It will also be useful to team participants in subsequent phases of the project.

DECISION POINTS

Throughout the process of developing an effective Web strategy, there are many important decisions to be made. But none is as important and potentially risky as the go versus no-go decision. These days, most companies have already made some type of commitment to a Web presence, so we're not talking about the decision of whether or not to have a Web site. We're talking about the decisions regarding whether to use the Web as a vehicle by which to build your business and your relationships with your markets—whether to adopt a Whole Experience approach. How to plan and execute a Whole Experience Web site is the focus of subsequent steps of the Whole Experience road map. But, at this step, the commitment to go forward and create a Web business strategy is the key decision from which numerous other decisions stem.

Adopting a Whole Experience approach is not a binary decision—that is, it isn't really as simple as a go–versus–no-go decision. It's really about how far you go. How far do your customers want you to go? How far are your competitors pushing you to go? The risk of *not* going forward may be greater than the risks of going forward.

The opportunity analysis should identify the "must-have" elements of the Web strategy in your marketplace. Based on your comprehensive review of current market practices, the analysis should outline opportunities your company has to differentiate itself with a Web presence. It should also suggest what the business objectives of the site might be—given the market conditions, as well as the strategic imperative, the level of priority, and the timing implications for maintaining company competitiveness.

A concern that always arises in the early phases of Web strategy development entails questioning what the financial investment is going to be. While this is a reasonable concern to have, total expenditures for the project cannot typically be comprehended at this step—an unpopular but true fact. Achieving total budget certainty is desirable at this stage, but it is not realistic because there are simply too many open issues that could dramatically impact the total necessary funding.

In fact, committing to a budget at this juncture can be counterproductive, because there have been no projections of what the Web strategy may yield in terms of new and retained business or in cost savings. Therefore, decisions to restrict budgets at this point can be detrimental to creating the best strategy for your business survival. It is more realistic to determine the required budget during the technical specifications development of step 4, so that the project has enough funding for you to reach the point of being able to comprehend the total resource requirements. Many experienced e-business executives will tell you that building their Web presence took much more time and money than they ever imagined at the outset.

OUTPUT

The resulting output from your company's efforts during the opportunity assessment phase is compiled in a formal document that can be delivered in both report and presentation format. The report should cover these basic components:

- Competitor review
- Customer assessment: level of Web access, preference, use in other categories
- Distribution channel assessment

- Level of urgency/priority
- Tradeoff analysis: go versus no-go
- Recommendations on best path strategy, timeline, next-step team structure
- Recommended budget to complete step 4, the technical specifications step

The report should be presented to executive management to seek a commitment to the next step. Executive management should then appoint the team for step 2, business strategy development. In addition, executive management must communicate its decision to go forward to the parties who need to know rather than saddling the appointed team with politically intensive internal education.

Target team members for the business strategy development phase should include individuals from the opportunity assessment team along with executives from each of the operational areas that could potentially be affected by a Web strategy. This usually includes sales, corporate marketing, channel marketing, product management, fulfillment, and customer service management. In addition, because step 2 includes a lot of project, company, and departmental P&Ls analysis, a member of the finance team is also a key player in this phase.

One cautionary note: While the list of team members is somewhat long, it is imperative to keep the total number down to a manageable size so that meetings and decisions can quickly be concluded. Team members should be given at least partial relief from their normal job duties or have their priorities shuffled so that they are able to perform this important job function with high-quality energy.

Step Two: Business Strategy Development

The end goal of the business-strategy development phase is to create a comprehensive business plan complete with objectives, required actions, organizational structures, etc. Getting to that end goal—producing an astute, ready-for-action business plan—requires the evaluation of both external and internal data.

Data Required

You have a head start in data collection for step 2, because much of the external data needed for business-strategy development was completed in the opportunity analysis phase. Assuming the team did a thorough job of understanding the market requirements, this information can be pressed into service immediately as part of the business plan. If holes were discovered in the information presented as part of the opportunity analysis, then the void should be filled in this phase.

The more intensive data collection and analysis efforts in this phase are focused on internal data. The team must have access to operating and strategic planning information, such as:

- Current and projected P&Ls
- Current and projected cost-center budgets for IT and marketing
- Cost analysis of key functional areas such as fulfillment and support
- Sales force and channel compensation models
- Current business processes and work flows
- Product profitability analysis
- Customer sales and profitability analysis

Decision Points

There are myriad decisions in creating a rigorous Web business plan. These decisions will concern:

- Enabling Consumption Cycle functions
- Focusing business objectives
- Offering products
- Delivering the brand promise
- Building direct customer relationships
- Improving business processes

Consumption Cycle Function Decisions

At the most fundamental level, there remains key question that must be answered: What aspects of the Consumption Cycle should we address with our Web site? Some companies make the mistake of thinking of the Web merely as a storefront—an alternative distribution channel. While the Web is an important commerce channel for many companies, there's more to it than selling. You should ask yourself:

- Should customers be permitted to shop and find information about my company, our products, services, and employment opportunities on the Web site?
- Should people be enabled and encouraged to buy my company's products or services on the Web? Should it be through the company's Web site where they make the sales transactions, or through someone else's, such as a channel partner or a portal—or both?
- If it is someone else's site, what do I need to do to make that happen?
- Should customers be enabled to inquire about delivery status and track product shipments through the Web site?
- Should customer support services be offered via the site?

There are a plethora of subquestions that accompany each of these top-line issues. But the business plan must specifically address what the company will do in response to each of these key aspects of the Consumption Cycle, and for whom. This leads to another fundamental decision in the business strategy development phase: The plan must pinpoint who the target visitors are—suspects, prospects, customers, partners, employees, investors, channels, etc.

BUSINESS-OBJECTIVE DECISIONS

There remains another set of business strategy decisions that determine the business objectives of the site. With your site, do you aim to:

- Expand into new markets?
- Generate sales leads?
- Increase sales? Of what products? At what price?
- Build direct relationships with customers?
- Attract and acquire new customers?

- Retain existing customers? Increase customer satisfaction?
- Shorten the sales cycle?
- Decrease business-cycle costs?

Each of these questions stimulates a raft of issues that must be analyzed and generates multiple other questions that must be resolved. For example, if you plan to attract new customers, you must flesh out:

- Who they are
- The size of the opportunity
- The value proposition and benefits you uniquely offer to your target markets
- Why the Web has made them a potential target
- How you reach them through the Web and the associated costs

Some companies hope to increase sales through their Web presence but don't have a clear picture of what is realistic to expect. A critical reality to keep in mind is that the increase in sales and customer retention will be directly correlated to how you plan to drive traffic to the site, the quality of the site experience, and the Consumption Cycle functions enabled on the site. It is somewhat of a chicken and egg problem. If the company underfunds the site and its promotion, your Web sales will suffer. But in the planning phase, it is difficult to know how much is the right amount to spend to reach target business objectives. That's one of the reasons why prototyping the site and testing the response to the prototype is critical to solidifying its success metrics.

Product-Line Decisions

Another decision relates to what products you intend to sell on the Web and what the pricing strategy will be. As discussed in chapter 3, toe-in-the-water strategies that offer limited or price-disadvantaged products can result in failure for many companies. In the business plan, you must address head-on the products and services that will be made available on the Web and commit to overcoming the strategic conflicts that will follow.

BRAND-PROMISE DECISIONS

Another aspect to developing the value proposition strategy is addressing the brand promise you make to customers. Your team should be deciding on the following:

- What actions might we take to ensure that both our traditional and online brand strategies coincide? Is it possible to create a single strategy that spans both traditional and new media?
- How do we create an online value proposition that consistently fulfills and delivers our brand promise?
- How can we build trusting relationships between ourselves and our customers and increase brand loyalty when the Web is the medium of interaction? Are we committed to making the required investments to build our brand on the Web?

CUSTOMER-RELATIONSHIP DECISIONS

Many companies see the Web as the first opportunity they've had to develop a direct relationship with their customers. The Web provides an exciting opportunity to know who your customers are and to build a rapport with them. These companies have relied on distribution channels to move products to market and therefore have never had much contact with their end-user customer. But taking the step to develop direct relationships with customers, however, will probably create chaos in the distribution channel. Companies should comprehend the full implications of this strategy on their distribution channel relationships.

A primary reason to build direct relationships with customers via the Web is to be able to track and improve customer satisfaction. One of the disadvantages to selling strictly through distribution, instead of direct, is the lack of customer feedback on how well you are serving the ultimate end-user customer's needs. Used properly, the Web is a vehicle that not only allows you to build a direct rapport with your customers, but it also allows you to keep pace with how you are doing in meeting their expectations.

Business-Process Decisions

One of the popular objectives touted in the media and by other business books entails using the Web to decrease business process costs. Creating objectives that focus on taking costs out of the business cycle requires an astute analysis of the operational data listed above, applying the "best-practices" knowledge gained in the opportunity analysis phase, and understanding how things are done in your company today. For example, many companies have experienced dramatic savings in customer support because many questions are handled online by making more information available to customers, which curbs the number of questions answered via telephone support. However, other companies are noticing some frustration within their customer base because customers expect to have questions answered online very rapidly. Yet, many customer support organizations are not equipped to handle Web-based support questions.

In this example, knowing how your company works, what kind of support customers require, the number of calls handled per month, and a headcount of employees in place to handle the tasks are all key data points in setting business objectives to take costs out of customer support processes. This is an area that has paid off for many companies and is one that warrants special attention from the business strategy development team.

There are many examples of ways companies have achieved significant cost savings and created competitive advantage using the Internet. We have talked about some dramatic examples in this book. These companies succeed because they confront an important strategic issue—understanding their true core competencies and identifying areas where they should partner with other companies to augment those competencies and streamline business processes.

Output

The output of this phase is the Whole Experience business plan. Like any business plan, it has core elements, including:

- Situation overview: recaps findings from opportunity analysis
- Business objectives
- Target audiences/markets
- Definition of the Whole Experience: key Consumption Cycle functions addressed by the site
- Profitability/cost-impact analysis
- Resource requirements: organization, leadership, time
- Timeline

Step Three: Functional Strategy Development

The business plan from step 2 provides the framework for the site strategy. It also provides substantial intelligence about what the market requires, what the company hopes to gain, and what fundamental aspects of the Consumption Cycle will be addressed with the site strategy. The next step is to flesh out how your company will use the Web to create a Whole Experience for your target audience that will differentiate your company in your market.

DATA REQUIRED

At this point on the road map, it is time to look again to the outside world, learn more deeply about what the customer wants from the site experience, and use the information about company business processes. You have already decided whether you will sell, track, and support products with your Web site. How you perform those functions is defined in this stage.

Attaining a better understanding of what customers want requires some direct-contact research. Whether you gather this data in focus groups or personal interviews, the fundamental things you need to know about customers are:

- What do they want to do on your site?
- What are the alternative ways of performing those activities?
- How do they learn about Web sites they frequent?
- What type of content do they prefer if they are shopping? What are they most likely to read?
- What do they want to buy from you?

- What method of payment do they prefer? Do they use credit cards? If they are a business, what are the purchasing procedures that must be accommodated?
- What are their concerns about security?
- What are their attitudes about privacy and providing personal information?
- Do they want to be able to track product shipments?
- How do they prefer to be supported? How do they currently receive customer service? How well does it work? Where can it be improved? What are their response time requirements for support?

You also need to know more about your company's business processes beyond what you assessed to set business objectives. Here you need to understand the internal work flow and business processes that are currently in use so that you can comprehend how the Web will impact them. As we have mentioned throughout this book, for the Web to be successful it must be integrated into the company's normal business processes. It should become the priority of many people throughout the organization to make the Web a component of successfully conducted business. Therefore, the functional strategy needs to address all elements of the company. These include:

- For product and service information, how is content currently developed, who is involved, and what systems are they using for writing, designing, and publishing? How often does the content need to change?
- What are the internal graphic and design competencies?
- In sales, how are transactions handled? Do customers provide credit cards, or do they use purchase orders and invoices? What role does the salesperson or sales channel play? How will that change if the site is performing sales-related tasks?
- What competencies are possessed by the IT department for handling a sophisticated Web presence? What technology platforms are currently in use? What software products does the group know how to use?
- What can be leveraged from the existing Web site?

DECISION POINTS

Decisions must be made in three key areas: definition of the experience, design of business processes, and resources needed to go forward.

DEFINITION OF THE EXPERIENCE

To define the site experience means that you have to decide what visitors will be able to do on your site and to anticipate how your company's image is reflected based on that experience. From a functional perspective, that translates into decisions such as:

- How will enabled Consumption Cycle functions actually work? That is, how will customers make purchases, what forms of payment will you accept, and what steps are involved in the transaction process?
- What will the organizing principle of the site be? Customer segment, product, functional area?
- Will personalization and profile information be used to tune the experience?
- What will make the site dynamic? What will the key hook be that will compel visitors to continue to come back?

DESIGN OF BUSINESS PROCESSES

Every key aspect of the Consumption Cycle has a corollary process that has to be developed to make the site a reality and to integrate the Web into normal business processes. Some of these include:

- Forwarding and handling generated leads
- Developing and updating content
- Conducting transactions and methods of payment
- Tracking product
- Supporting customers

RESOURCES FOR DEVELOPMENT

Another key decision will be to select who will be on the development team. This involves assessing your company's own internal competencies and deciding whether you have the needed talent or whether you have to hire an outside vendor. There are several categories of competencies you must consider:

- Content development
- Graphic design and user interface
- Software development
- Finance and administration operations
- Outbound marketing
- Business development: to strike deals with partners, portals, etc.

We recommend that work groups be assigned to move forward into the specific aspects of prototyping and that one management group oversee the operations of the work groups. These groups should include:

- Executive management group: makes strategic decisions about the site, reports to senior management on prototyping progress, and approves and tracks budget.
- Technical development: responsible for technical creation of the site.
- Graphic design: responsible for look and feel of the site, navigation design, and user interface.
- Content development: responsible for creation of site content—from the shortest sentence to the longest document. This includes marketing, sales, and support content. Therefore, someone from each functional area that is affected by the site should be represented in this group.

OUTPUT

The decisions made in step 3 culminate in a site requirements document, which becomes the guideline for the teams responsible for creating the prototype site. The document, which is discussed in more detail in chapter 6, specifies these components:

- Web site objectives
- Functional goals and requirements
- Navigation
- Graphic design specifications
- Content updating
- Prototyping team: internal and external resources

Step Four: Technical Specifications

Before the site can be prototyped, the project must be technologically defined and the appropriate technology solutions must be selected to create the site. This is the objective of the technical specifications phase of the Whole Experience road map. Creating the technical specifications document is the responsibility of the technical development team, the components of which are discussed briefly in chapter 6.

DATA REQUIRED

The site requirements document created during step 3 provides details of the site functionality and serves as a framework for specifying the required technology. This critical information will guide you in selecting the right technology. There are many examples: If the site requirements document calls for content to be contributed by people throughout the organization and for that content to be updated frequently, a distributed content publishing system is needed. If the content is to be dynamically generated based on the site visitor's preferences and past behavior, then profiling and dynamic content generation and management solutions will be needed. If your customers want to make purchases using credit cards, then encryption technology will be needed to ensure secure transactions. If customers will be able to buy multiple products in one session on your site, you will need shopping cart technology.

As discussed in chapter 6, the range of technology solutions from which to choose can be mind-boggling, not just in terms of sorting out the options, but in substantiating the claims of technology vendors. The technical development team needs to take numerous steps in its data gathering, including the following:

- Assess what technology is used in-house in terms of hardware, operating systems, database software, financials, and so on
- Spend time talking with representatives from other companies to learn what they are successfully using and get advice from IT and Web consultants

- Assess the skills available in-house as well as the availability of knowledgeable talent on the open market—people who know how to use the selected technology

Decision Points

After completing its factfinding research, the team will typically submit RFPs (requests for proposal) to technology vendors and/or consultants to solicit proposals for solutions and services. If you require assistance in several areas, such as graphic design and technical development, you will probably need different RFPs, because often one service vendor does not have the full range of competencies needed to be a one-stop shop. For reference, a suggested RFP outline is provided in chapter 6.

Members of the entire team should participate in the vendors' presentations of their proposals, as many times the decisions are not solely based on technical or graphic design merits. These projects require productive working relationships, and vendors should be selected based on trust and accountability—not just Web prowess.

The decisions in this phase are complex and far-reaching. Investments in technology solutions can range into the millions of dollars. Selecting the right vendors can make the difference between outrageous success and utter failure. And the implications in terms of maintenance and growth are significant. Keeping these things in mind, the questions you need answered include:

- Are vendors willing to work as part of a team with other vendors?
- Does your current site development team know the software? If not, what will it take for team members to learn about it and become proficient with it?
- Are there trained professionals available who know the chosen software, not just today, but in the years to come?
- Is the software-solution provider a stable company? Will it be in business three years from now, when you'll still need product support? Are the components involved compatible

with legacy systems? Will your internal IT department have to integrate the solution in order to interoperate?
- Does the software run on an industry standard hardware platform?
- What is the assumed amount of site traffic that this technology can handle? What happens if the traffic doubles, triples, quadruples?
- Will you be dependent on a service provider to help maintain and expand the site? If so, what are the long-term budget implications and risks?

OUTPUT

The technical specifications document lays out detailed requirements of the site in terms of software, hardware required, development phases, benchmarks, and budgets. It serves as one of the key guidelines for the prototyping phase of the project. Primary sections of the document are:

- Hardware and software platforms, including:
  Specified operating system
  Web server
  Application server
  User profiling and dynamic HTML page generation
      software
  Database software
  Content publishing software
  Document management software
- Registration system
- Customer database design
- Back-office systems integration
- Security and firewall
- Legacy content conversion
- Target browsers
- Entitlements (i.e., rules that dictate which visitors get access to what content)
- Dynamic page generation
- Systems administration

- Search technology
- Reporting mechanisms
- Special networking requirements, such as virtual private networks

Step Five: Prototype Development

Prototyping a site is a critical phase in the road map, but one that some companies may mistakenly consider unnecessary. We strongly urge you to build a prototype for several reasons—and most of them relate to money. Prototyping allows you to try out concepts to see how well they fit customers' requirements— before spending too much money. It allows you to test technology solutions and the development teams to ensure that the selected technology is able to adequately be scaled and that the development teams are appropriately skilled. It also gives you the required data to refine your functional and technical specifications and budget for the full-blown site. Skipping the prototype phase can lead to unfocused efforts, uncontrolled spending, and off-the-mark site experiences.

The final, key element of the prototyping phase is user testing. Before moving on, companies should always test site responses among target customers in a controlled usability lab setting in order to ensure the site approach works the way it was intended.

Data Required

The combined data from the site requirements and technical specifications documents provides guidance regarding the prototyping effort. The site requirements document should be very specific about what the site should enable from a features and functions perspective. The technical specifications document should outline the technology required for prototyping.

Decision Points

While many decisions have been made in the specifications documents, myriad decisions are made on a daily basis during the prototyping phase. Some of these decisions are about the details of the Web site experience: navigational schemes, personalization implementation, adapting the brand identity in an electronic form, the personality of the site, and page designs. Other decisions relate to work processes, such as content development processes and content sourcing or licensing of external content.

When the prototype is ready, it should be subjected to live testing from target users in a controlled setting, such as one-on-one interviews or focus groups in usability labs. In these settings, participants are allowed to move through the site and react to the experience. Careful analysis of customer and prospect reactions can reveal the specific areas that need to be refined prior to the next phase—site development. Findings from the usability testing should be presented to all members of the teams.

At this point, it is important that you realize that refinement is an ongoing process. It is during this step that many companies learn what continuous improvement really means.

OUTPUT

Prototyping yields a number of significant output components, all of which are documented in the site development plan, including:

- A design that is ready for a full build, complete with navigational templates approved by the executive management team
- The underlying technology decisions that have been confirmed (e.g., content publishing platforms, e-commerce solutions, customer database, and profiling and personalization
- The content resources that have been earmarked for all aspects of the experience—product data, sales policies, and customer support information
- The fulfillment procedures, which have been defined
- The development partners or internal team selected
- The internal ownership and management of the site, which has been formalized
- A budget that has been defined and approved

At this juncture, it is critical that organizational buy-in and executive approval has been gained. There will be many bumps in the road along the way. It is wise to eliminate as many problems as possible before moving into the intense site development phase.

Step Six: Site Development

Once the prototype meshes with customers' expectations and commitments have been made for all of the components in the site development plan, the site development begins in earnest. At this point, several aspects of site development work parallel together, including:

- Technical development: programming of the site software
- Design implementation: designing all of the pages using the approved graphic and navigational standards
- Content development: creating and acquiring the content necessary to fill the site's pages
- Marketing strategy: designing the methods that will lead traffic to the site

Data Required

At this juncture, a formal set of documents should be assembled that will serve as a resource to all members of the site development team. This includes all of the work that has been documented to date, including the:

- Opportunity analysis
- Whole Experience business plan
- Site requirements document
- Technical specifications document
- Usability research findings
- Site development plan

Decision Points

Throughout the site development processes, many decisions will be made that will ultimately shape the Web site experience of the end-user. As an executive manager, you will not be able to be involved with every minute decision, but it is important that you and the executive team be closely involved with the progress of each of the teams. The requirements of a project like Web site development are often difficult to comprehend at the outset, especially in terms of time and budget.

Teams need to be managed to ensure that timelines and spending are kept in check. We recommend having regularly scheduled project-update meetings, during which leaders from each of the four development teams report on progress, issues, and completion status.

While all of the development teams have a critical-path role, the most perilous to control and manage is the technical development aspect. This is because the tasks are very complex and difficult, and it is new territory for most people involved. It helps for the executive to understand the core activities that the team will be performing. The basic steps that the technical development team will take involve coding the underlying data structures that allow the various parts of the Consumption Cycle to function. These include registration databases, e-commerce software, content database software, fulfillment, shipment tracking, and customer services. Many iterations and tests will be required during this phase.

Specific milestones, complete with deadlines, need to be established for technical development. This area can often get in trouble, and in extreme cases derail the project. Some suggested milestones include:

- Frequent test data loads
- Simulations of transactions and customer data pulls
- Checkoffs with product marketing and customer marketing to assure data can be modified and extracted
- Check-offs with customer service for integration in current processes
- Close and frequent contact with graphic/UI and content development teams

Another important decision area in this phase is developing the customer acquisition strategy—how you attract visitors to your site. The types of decisions you make at this juncture are both strategic and tactical. From a strategic perspective, you should consider if you need to develop partnerships with other companies, which may attract the interest of your target customers and may be in a position to influence them to visit your site. The best known examples of these types of partnerships are portal sites such as America Online, Yahoo!, Excite, and NetCenter. In addition, a concept known as vertical portals has become popular, whereby sites specialize in a wide array of topical areas such as healthcare, small business, children, or travel. These sites may potentially already have visitors that fit the profile of your target customer and thus may be a contact through which you could acquire customers.

Because of the lead times in ramping marketing programs, it is important to begin planning for marketing of the site while it is in development, so that when it is ready to launch you do not lose any time. Important customer acquisition decisions are:

- What vehicles should be used to drive traffic to the site? Advertising, public relations, direct mail? It has been found that traditional ways of communicating with target customers may also be appropriate to attract them to your site.
- What will it cost to drive traffic to the site? Traditional marketing vehicles are expensive, and Web budgets are often incremental to existing marketing budgets.
- How can existing marketing efforts and expenditures be leveraged to attract customers to the site?

OUTPUT

The final phases of site development—that is, before the site is considered operational and ready for public launch—are alpha and beta testing. An alpha test involves full functionality testing on a limited data load. In addition, alpha tests should include full usability testing by an outside party. At this juncture, your team will be too personally invested to perform unbiased user testing internally.

After these two steps, other actions occur, including:

- Functionality and design refinement, such as user interface and navigation
- Full content loading
- Schedule for beta launch
- Internal communications strategy
- Partner buy-in and communications

After alpha testing is completed and refinements are made based on that testing, the site is ready for beta launch. Often beta launches involve allowing people from outside of the development teams to use the site and give feedback on glitches, bugs, and other areas where refinement is needed. The schedule should allow for adequate time to fix problems discovered in beta testing.

In these final phases of development, the marketing team should be focusing on the customer data and competitive environment in order to develop the Web site launch strategy. The launch strategy should include these elements:

- Marketing objectives
- Strategic alliance/portal deals
- Public relations, utilizing customer and trade press
- Advertising, using online and traditional vehicles
- Ongoing customer acquisition strategy
- Loyalty/retention program development
- Budget/Success metrics

Step Seven: Operational Implementation

After all of the work outlined previously in this chapter is done, it is a happy day when the site is actually implemented. But the task is not complete. Managing the site as a strategic business vehicle is critical. You will require a solid, ongoing Web site management team to keep the site compelling, vibrant, and effective.

DATA REQUIRED

It is important to track site traffic and to have robust reporting mechanisms to measure how visitors are responding to the site, and standard reports should be created for management review. There are many software products that enable Web site tracking.

One of the reasons why tracking is key is that it ensures that your systems have the capability to handle the site traffic. Too many companies have underestimated Web site traffic and have not been able to serve all of their visitors, which resulted in lost business. Management should focus on tracking Web site traffic and capacity with the same vigilance as tracking sales and manufacturing output.

Decision Points

Once the site is implemented, you will be faced with many decisions regarding how to make the site more effective, how to make it more meaningful in building your market position, and how to leverage it to decrease business-cycle costs. In making these decisions, we recommend thinking of the Web as an opportunity to do a better job for your customers. Use it to seek ways to build stronger relationships with them.

Output

After the site is implemented, many ideas on ways to refine and improve it will emerge. To manage the effort, it should be required that the Web-site management team develops a strategic operating plan in the same business cycles as are required for other departments and P&Ls in your company. A Web business plan should include such standard components as objectives, planned improvements, required budgets, and timelines.

Step Eight: Ongoing Refinement

This is the area that makes us aware of the fact that, on the Web, no project is ever really finished. Technology is changing so rapidly and customers are evolving their preferences so quickly that change becomes a required core competency.

Data Required

The data required for ongoing refinement includes a periodic assessment of customer requirements and how well your site fits those requirements, an understanding of the competitive land-scape, and internal audits for business process effectiveness.

DECISION POINTS

There are a plethora of ongoing decisions that must be made, many of them relating to business processes. Processes that require action include:

- Content updates
- Ongoing site functionality development
- Regular user interface testing
- Quarterly customer check-ins
- Competitive analysis

We advise that you have at least quarterly and perhaps monthly reviews of the site metrics, when decisions are made about site performance, implementation of new functionality, and customer feedback. Web site metrics should be reported in the company's normal business tracking formats.

OUTPUT

The output required from this phase is an ongoing plan for site upgrades, functionality improvements, and planned extensions, as well as a Web business plan. The Web team should work with a documented production schedule so that progress can be tracked and priorities established.

Conclusion

It is clear that there are myriad of actions and decisions to be made in the process of developing a strategic Web presence. The Whole Experience road map presented in this chapter provides guidance, but be aware that the road is bumpy and is constantly changing course. The Web represents a new way of doing business, the ripple effect of which will be significantly be felt throughout your company. Ongoing executive direction is imperative for success. Bon voyage.

Notes

CHAPTER 1

1. "Predictability: Does the Flap of a Butterfly's Wings in Brazil Set Off a Tornado in Texas?" a paper written by Edward Lorenz in 1979.
2. We interviewed David Perry, founder and CEO of Chemdex Corporation, via phone and e-mail.
3. We interviewed Darrell Ticehurst, president of InsWeb, via phone and e-mail.
4. We attended the 1998 Spotlight Conference and heard Neil Weintraut, a partner at 21st Century Internet Partners, comment about doing business online.
5. Dataquest, Inc. press release (29 January 1999).
6. C/NET News.com (8 January 1999).
7. We interviewed Chris Sinton, director of Cisco Connection, in person and via phone and e-mail.
8. Cognitiative, Inc. "Pulse of the Customer" research reports, December 1998 and April 1999 editions.

CHAPTER 2

1. We attended the 1998 Spotlight Conference and heard Tony Levitan, president of E-greetings Network, comment about doing business online.
2. We interviewed Ned Hoyt, cofounder and CEO of iOwn.com, via phone and e-mail.
3. We interviewed Chuck Harstad, vice president of corporate marketing at 3M, via phone and e-mail.
4. We attended the 1998 Spotlight Conference and heard Robert Olson, cofounder of Virtual Vineyards, comment about Internet security.
5. Theodore Levitt, *The Marketing Imagination* (New York: Free Press, 1986).

6. We attended the 1998 Spotlight Conference and heard Alan Fisher, cofounder and chief technology officer at ONSALE, comment about Internet business.
7. John Simons and Douglas A. Blackmon, "Online Shopping Lifts Delivery Concerns' Volume," *Wall Street Journal* (30 December 1998).
8. We interviewed Robert Langer, director of Dell Online, via phone and e-mail.
9. We interviewed Pamela Roberts, senior director of e-business for Symantec Corporation, via phone and e-mail.
10. We interviewed RealSelect's CEO Stuart Wolff via phone and e-mail.

Chapter 3

1. David Einstein, "Egghead Cracks the Net," the *San Francisco Chronicle* (15 July 1998).
2. We interviewed Tom Panelas, director of corporate communications for Encyclopaedia Britannica, via e-mail.
3. We attended a seminar entitled, "Using the Web for Greater Customer Satisfaction at a Lower Cost," held at the Internet Commerce Expo, Los Angeles Convention Center (22–25 September 1998). We heard Yvonne Schneider, a representative for American Express Corporate Services Interactive, talk about her company's experience doing business online.
4. We interviewed Robert Rodin, president and CEO of Marshall Industries, via phone and e-mail.
5. We interviewed Barry Peters, director of relationship marketing for ONSALE, via phone and e-mail.
6. Kimberly Weisul, "eBay Launches Anti-Fraud Measures," *Inter@ctive Week Online* (2 February 1999).
7. We interviewed Kevin Derella, franchise development manager for 1-800-Flowers, via e-mail.
8. Joseph Tripodi, executive vice president of global marketing for MasterCard International, as quoted in The American Marketing Association Special Report on Trends and Forces Shaping the Future of Marketing (1998).
9. We attended the 1998 Spotlight Conference and heard Barry Diller, CEO of USA Networks, comment on marketing and advertising via the Internet.

Chapter 4

1. Robert Kuttner, "The Net: A Market Too Perfect for Profit," *BusinessWeek* (11 May 1998).
2. Various press releases from E*TRADE: August 16 and 19, 1998; January 15, 22, and 29, 1999.
3. Megan Barnett, "Why Macy's.com Won't Sell Levi's," the *Industry Standard* (23 November 1998).

4. Jacob Ward, "Macy's.com Relaunches . . . ," the *Industry Standard* (18 November 1998).
5. Harry Beckwith, *Selling the Invisible* (New York: Warner Books, 1997).
6. Amazon.com's CEO Jeff Bezos, as quoted in the *New York Times* article, "Beyond Books, but Sticking to the Basics," by Saul Hansell (12 October 1998).

CHAPTER 5

1. R. L. Daft and A. Y. Lewin, "Where Are the Theories for the New Organizational Forms?" *Organizational Science* 4 (1993): i–vi.
2. We interviewed Anthony Sanchez, senior manager of Internet programs and development at Oracle Support Services, in person and via phone and e-mail.
3. We interviewed 3M's vice president of corporate marketing, Chuck Harstad, via phone and e-mail.
4. We interviewed Jim Radford, Internet marketing services manager for 3M, via phone and e-mail.

CHAPTER 6

1. "The Emerging Digital Economy," report published by the United States Department of Commerce, 1998.
2. Rebecca Quick, "Gawkers or Shoppers? Selling Bras on the Web," the *Wall Street Journal* (29 December 1998).
3. Ibid.
4. Ibid.
5. We interviewed Aaron Downey, president and CEO of roundpeg, in person and via phone and e-mail.
6. *Wall Street Journal* (29 December 1998).
7. We interviewed Phil Gibson, director of interactive marketing at National Semiconductor, via phone and e-mail.

CHAPTER 7

1. "Global Internet Project," a study published by GIP Internet Today and Tomorrow, 1998.
2. We interviewed Deborah Tyroler, senior Web strategist at International Communications, via phone and e-mail.
3. We interviewed Kennedy A. Brooks, an attorney and currently executive vice president of global planning and development for NETEQ Corporation, via phone and e-mail.
4. Kimberley A. Strassel, "If There's Something Rotten in Denmark, Mickey Denies All Guilt," the *Wall Street Journal* (12 January 1999).
5. "Framework for Global Electronic Commerce," report published by the United States Department of Commerce, 1997.

6. *KPMG Global Tax News*—June 1997 edition; July 1997 edition; November 1997 edition; February 1998 edition; and the June 1998 edition.
7. We interviewed Ruthanne Feinberg, manager of the electronic commerce division of the French Trade Commission, in person and via phone and e-mail.
8. We interviewed Jim Codrea, Controller for Lehigh Valley Safety Shoes, via phone.
9. We interviewed Ricardo Garcia Zetina, director of marketing and Channels for Centura Software de Mexico, via phone.

ADDITIONAL SOURCES

[Author/Editor?]. "Doing Business in the Internet Age," *BusinessWeek's* annual report on information technology (22 June 1998).

Benjamin, R. and R. Wigand. "Electronic Markets and Virtual Value Chains on the Information Highway," *Sloan Management Review* (Winter 1995), pp. 62–72.

Canedy, Dana. "Shopping for Toys without the Kids," the *New York Times* (27 July 1998).

Sarkar, M. B. et al. "Intermediaries and Cybermediaries: A Continuing Role for Mediating Players in the Electronic Marketplace." *Journal of Computer-Mediated Communication* 1, no. 3 (1996).

Sinton, Peter. "Banking on the Web," the *San Francisco Chronicle* (24 August 1998).

Wilder, Clinton and Justin Hibbard. "Pushing Outside the Enterprise," *Information Week* (4 August 1997).

Index

Books from Allworth Press

Money Secrets of the Rich and Famous by Michael Reynard (hardcover, 6¼ x 9¼, 256 pages, $24.95)

Your Living Trust and Estate Plan: How to Maximize Your Family's Assets and Protect Your Loved Ones, Second Edition by Harvey J. Platt (softcover, 6 x 9, 304 pages, $14.95)

The Retirement Handbook: How to Maximize Your Assets and Protect Your Quality of Life by Carl W. Battle (softcover, 6 x 9, 256 pages, $18.95)

The Trademark Guide: A Friendly Guide for Protecting and Profiting from Trademarks by Lee Wilson (softcover, 6 x 9, 192 pages, $18.95)

The Copyright Guide: A Friendly Guide for Protecting and Profiting from Copyrights by Lee Wilson (softcover, 6 x 9, 192 pages, $18.95)

The Patent Guide: A Friendly Guide to Protecting and Profiting from Patents by Carl W. Battle (softcover, 6 x 9, 224 pages, $18.95)

The Law (In Plain English)® for Small Businesses, Third Edition by Leonard DuBoff (softcover, 6 x 9, 256 pages, $19.95)

The Internet Publicity Guide: How to Maximize Your Marketing and Promotion in Cyberspace by V. A. Shiva (softcover, 6 x 9, 224 pages, $18.95)

The Internet Research Guide, Revised Edition by Timothy K. Maloy (softcover, 6 x 9, 208 pages, $18.95)

The Business of Multimedia by Nina Schulyer (softcover, 6 x 9, 240 pages, $19.95)

The Secret Life of Money: How Money Can Be Food for the Soul by Tad Crawford (softcover, 5½ x 8½ , 304 pages, $14.95)

Old Money: The Mythology of Wealth in America, Expanded Edition by Nelson W. Aldrich. Jr. (softcover, 6 x 9, 340 pages, $16.95)

Writing for Interactive Media: The Complete Guide by Jon Samsel and Darryl Wimberley (hardcover, 6 x 9, 320 pages, $19.95)

Writing.com: Creative Internet Strategies to Advance Your Writing Career by Moira Anderson Allen (softcover, 6 x 9, 256 pages, $16.95)

The Interactive Music Handbook: The Definitive Guide to Internet Music Strategies, Enhanced CD Production, and Business Development by Jodi Summers (softcover, 6 x 9, 296 pages, $19.95)

Please write to request our free catalog. To order by credit card, call 1-800-491-2808 or send a check or money order to Allworth Press, 10 East 23rd Street, Suite 210, New York, NY 10010. Include $5 for shipping and handling for the first book ordered and $1 for each additional book. Ten dollars plus $1 for each additional book if ordering from Canada. New York State residents must add sales tax.

To see our complete catalog on the World Wide Web, or to order online, you can find us at *www.allworth.com*.

Printed in the United States
1452700002B/27-28